THE SOCIOLOGICAL THEORY OF
C. WRIGHT MILLS

Kennikat Press

National University Publications

Series in American Studies

General Editor

James P. Shenton

Professor of History, Columbia University

JOSEPH A. SCIMECCA

THE SOCIOLOGICAL THEORY
of
C. WRIGHT MILLS

National University Publications
KENNIKAT PRESS   //   1977
Port Washington, N. Y.   //   London

Manufactured in the United States of America

Published by
Kennikat Press Corp.
Port Washington, N. Y./London

The author and publisher acknowledge, with thanks, the cooperation of the publishers listed below for permission to use excerpts from their books. *Character and Social Structure* by Hans Gerth and C. Wright Mills. © 1953 Harcourt Brace Jovanovich, Inc.; *Power, Politics and People: The Collected Essays of C. Wright Mills,* Irving L. Horowitz, ed. © 1964 Oxford University Press; "The Failure of American Sociology" by Dennis Wrong in *Commentary,* Nov. 1959; "'The Power Elite': Comment on Criticism" by C. Wright Mills in *Dissent,* Winter, 1957; "The Dragons of Marxism" by Irving L. Horowitz in *The American Scholar,* vol. 31, no. 4, Autumn, 1962. © 1962 the United Chapters of Phi Beta Kappa; *The Nature and Types of Sociological Theory* by Don Martindale. © 1960 Houghton Mifflin Co.; "Marxism and Science" by Al Szymanski, and "Pre-Marxian Marxism: A Critique of Szymanski's 'Marxism and Science'" by Richard Pozzuto in vol. 3, no. 3, Spring 1973, and vol. 3, no. 4, Summer 1973 in the *Insurgent Sociologist; The Sociology of Knowledge* by Stark Werner, 1958, Humanities Press for Routledge & Kegan Paul Ltd.; Essays in the *Theory of Society* by Ralf Dahrendorf. © 1968 Stanford University Press; *The Political Theory of John Dewey* by A. H. Somjee, New York: Teachers College Press, 1968; *Mind, Self and Society* by G. Herbert Mead. © 1934 University of Chicago Press; *New Directions in Sociological Theory* by Filmer, Phillipson, Silverman and Walsh. © 1973 M.I.T. Press; *The Coming Crisis of Western Sociology* by Alvin W. Gouldner. © 1970 Alvin W. Gouldner, Basic Books, Inc.; *C. Wright Mills and the Power Elite* compiled by G. William Domhoff and Hoyt B. Ballard. © 1968 Beacon Press; *Images of Man* by C. Wright Mills ed. © 1960 by C. Wright Mills, George Braziller, Inc.; *The Marxists* by C. Wright Mills. © 1962 C. Wright Mills, Dell Publishing Co.; *Pragmatic Philosophy,* Amelie Rorty ed. © 1966, Anchor Books.

Library of Congress Cataloging in Publication Data

Scimecca, Joseph.
    The sociological theory of C. Wright Mills.

    (Series in American studies) (National university publications)
        Bibliography: p.
        Includes index.
        1. Mills, Charles Wright. 2. Sociology.
    I. Title.
    HM22.U6M46   301'.092'4   76-18749
    ISBN 0-8046-9155-X

TO ELSIE AND KIRSTEN

PREFACE

This book takes an approach decidedly different from other interpretations of C. Wright Mills's sociology. It is my contention that Mills produced a fairly systematic sociology—a sociology based on a particular model. Mills was a practicing sociologist, and his radicalism stemmed from a structural perspective—not the other way around, as some would have us believe. This model must provide the starting point for any analysis of C. Wright Mills's sociological theory. This book revolves around the arguments for the existence and importance of Mills's model, both for those who consider themselves as working in the tradition of C. Wright Mills and for sociological theory in general.

In a work of this sort one incurs many debts, and therefore I can list only those who come most readily to mind. For their typing help, my gratitude to Cecilia Ormsby and Sharon Baron. Also, a thank you to those who read and commented on various stages of the manuscript: D. M. Azimi, Mark Berger, Robert Bierstedt, Bhopinda S. Bolaria, Margaret Donnelly, Francis X. Femminella, Peter Hopke, Roger Longo, Jerry S. Manaker, Richard Quinney, Harvey Segal, Dennis Van Essendelft, W. Paul Vogt, and Dennis H. Wrong. A special thanks to Mrs. Yaroslava Mills, who gave unselfishly of her time, provided access to Mills's unpublished works, and never was anything but cheerful and helpful even in the face of countless naïve questions about her late husband. The caveat that I alone am responsible for the interpretations in this book is exceedingly important given the nature of this work.

And lastly, I come to my wife, Elsie. To her, a thanks for just being Elsie. It is to her and our daughter Kirsten that this book is dedicated.

A different version of chapter five appeared in *The Review of Social Theory*, September 1974.

A final note: although a staunch supporter of sexual equality, I have, for purely stylistic reasons, used masculine referents throughout.

J. A. S.

Guilderland, New York

CONTENTS

THE SOCIOLOGICAL THEORY OF
C. WRIGHT MILLS

1

INTRODUCTION

Scholar and radical—C. Wright Mills played both roles during his lifetime. At a time when others went to great lengths to separate the two, Mills actively sought to combine them, unfortunately never quite succeeding. Many have dismissed Mills entirely for that failure, and misunderstandings have obscured his genuine accomplishments. It is part of the purpose of this book to clear up the misunderstandings and controversies that have distorted previous interpretations of Mills's sociology.

My position is that Mills's sociological theory is based upon a model of man and society which is an alternative to both structural-functional and conflict models. This model, which Mills called a general or "working model of a social system," is a synthesis of two divergent intellectual traditions—pragmatism and German sociology,[1] specifically Weberian sociology. It enabled Mills to "come face to face with the most important issue of political reflection—and of political action in our time: the problem of the historical agency of change, of the social and institutional means of structural change."[2] The model, then, should be the basis for any evaluation of the sociology of Mills, rather than his excursions into polemicism, or even his radical political stances. Though his actions were important and, given the period in which he took them, heroic, Mills was first and foremost a sociologist, and it is on this basis that he should be judged.

Mills defined the term *model* in a special sense, and I will follow his usage. His clearest statement of what constitutes a "working model of a social system" is found in his introduction to *Images of Man*, a work he edited in 1960, where he discussed why the early classical social scientists were still considered giants:

But how, it may be asked, can these men be so often wrong and yet remain so great? The answer lies, I think, in a single characteristic of their work: their "great ideas" consist of what might be called "models," in contrast to specific theories or detailed hypotheses. In these working models are contained statements of (1) the elements to which attention must be paid if we are to understand some particular feature of society or a society as a whole, and (2) the range of possible relations among these elements. The elements are not left merely to interact in some vague way. Rightly or wrongly, they are constructed in close and specific interconnection with one another, and causal weights are assigned to each. These imputed connections and weights of course are specific theories.

In short, the classic sociologists construct models of society and use them to develop a number of theories. What is important is the fact that neither the correctness nor the inaccuracy of any of these specific theories necessarily confirms or upsets the usefulness or the adequacy of the models. The models can be used for the construction of many theories. They can be used for correcting errors in theories made with their aid. And they are readily open: they can themselves be modified in ways to make them more useful as analytic tools and empirically closer to the run of fact.[3]

A model, as Mills uses the concept, is not true or false, it is simply a systematic inventory of elements. A theory, on the other hand, can be proved true or false in terms of causal weight and relations of the elements of the model.[4]

Mills, who considered himself an heir to the classical tradition in sociology, constructed such a model—one that corrected both the amorphous conception of social structure held by the pragmatists and Weber's deficient notion of personality formation.

Although this "working model" is implicit in almost all of Mills's works, his most precise articulation of the model is found in *Character and Social Structure* (1953), written with Hans Gerth,[5] and in *The Sociological Imagination* (1959). In *Character and Social Structure* Mills combines the social behaviorism of George Herbert Mead and John Dewey, which he had been exposed to as an undergraduate and a master's student in philosophy at the University of Texas, with a conception of social structure as an articulation of institutional orders. Mills takes pragmatism's social-structureless notion of personality formation and through an emphasis upon the roles individuals play in various institutions, shows how personality is molded by these institutional orders, and how these same institutional orders combine in any given society to form historical types of social structures. *The Sociological Imagination* is a refinement of the framework worked out in *Character and Social Structure*. The major difference between the two works is that *The Sociological Imagination* has less of an emphasis on personality formation and a greater stress on value judgments and activism. Content that he had worked out a viable system of personality formation in *Character and*

Social Structure, in subsequent works Mills concentrated more on objective factors, what he refered to as "the main drift" of historical and structural forces that are often impersonal and unrecognized by those who suffer their impact, and how the social scientist might intervene to offset their effect.

THE MODEL AND MILLS'S WRITINGS

The easiest way to understand Mills's sociological theory is to look at his writings as points on an almost chronological continuum—a continuum which starts out with an interest in pragmatism and slowly proceeds forward toward a synthesis with Weberian sociology.

Mills's early essays in the sociology of knowledge, written from 1939 to 1942, as well as his doctoral dissertation, "A Sociological Account of Pragmatism" (1942), published posthumously as *Sociology and Pragmatism: The Higher Learning in America* (1964), are steeped in pragmatism. His first published book, *The New Men of Power* (1948),[6] is also imbued with this philosophical system. It represents the pragmatist's emphasis upon action and shows how Mills accepted pragmatism's belief in "the power of man's intelligence to control his destiny."[7] Mills's essays written in the 1940's also point up the importance of pragmatism in his intellectual development in that they show his continued acceptance of the notion that reason leads to freedom—this in spite of a growing disenchantment with labor as an agent for historical change.

White Collar (1951) is at a further point on the continuum. Here Mills combines Weber's bureaucratic vision with the social behaviorist's theory of personality formation. Irving Louis Horowitz makes similar comments about Mills's early writings but differs with my interpretation of Mills's work after *White Collar.* According to Horowitz, Mills completely abandoned pragmatism as an intellectual framework, incorporating it only as a style of life.[8] Mills, I believe, never abandoned pragmatism but made it a part of his working model of a social system.

Character and Social Structure (1953) is next on the continuum. Here, as I stated before, Mills's working model approach is first articulated. Within its pages Mills combines the social basis of personality or character formation postulated by Mead, Dewey, and Peirce with the sociologist's notion of social structure and social constraint. This synthesis is arrived at by focusing upon the concept of social role, which is defined as "(1) units of conduct which by their recurrence stand out as regularities and (2) which are oriented to the patterns of others."[9] Man is envisioned as an historical creation and must be understood in terms of the roles he enacts and incorporates. These roles are in turn limited by the institutions into which the individual is born and in which he reaches adulthood. Five major orders—political, economic, military, kinship, and religious—form the skeletal structure of the total society. There are also several spheres of conduct which characterize all of the institutional orders. Mills considers symbols, technology, status, and education to be the four main spheres. The unity and composition of any social system have to do with the precise weight each institutional order carries and the ways in which they are related to each other. Order is, therefore, analyzed via the integration of institutional orders, and change is explained by focusing upon the historical shifts from one mode of integration to another. Mills's thesis of a power elite ruling America, for example, is an application of his model. *The Power Elite* is a theory of stratification seen in terms of the institutional integration of society. Here Mills is primarily interested in two things: (1) how American society at mid-century is integrated; and (2) how the individual is shaped by institutional orders in light of this integration.

Toward the latter part of his career, Mills began to vacillate between scholarship and activism, favoring the latter. Faced with the political reality of American society at mid-twentieth century, Mills became more and more a political radical, one who, to use his own words, "refuses to accept injustice as fate and whose refusal takes a political form."[10] Because he took this position and perhaps due also to the essential loneliness (and subsequent lack of feedback from colleagues) such a position entailed during the time Mills so appropriately labelled "the mindless years," his success was mixed. On the one hand, with the publication of *The Socio-logical Imagination,* Mills succeeded in raising serious questions about the underpinnings of the scientific status of sociology, a position that reached fruition in the 1960's and 1970's. And *The Marxists* (1962), his last book, is also a fine critique of both Marxism and liberalism, the twin cannons of twentieth-century political thought. Yet during this time, Mills also pro-duced *The Causes of World War III* (1958), and *Listen Yankee* (1960), which are his weakest books.

That Mills was not completely successful in his efforts to apply his framework cannot detract from its overall importance. What is important is the model itself. This historically based working model of a social system provides a rubric with which we can begin to answer the age-old questions of what holds society together and how man is related to this process. It takes on an even greater importance when we look at what is occurring in sociology today. Functionalism, which had been the major paradigmatic framework in sociology since the late 1930's, has entered a state of entropy.[11] Various other models—conflict theory, ethnomethodology, exchange theory, symbolic interactionism, phenomenological sociology, to mention the more important ones—are now vying with functionalism for primary status in sociology. Of these contenders, conflict theory, in particular the Marxist brand, is far and away the leading challenger. However, those conflict-oriented sociologists, for the most part younger and more radical than their functionalist counterparts, have not been able to reconcile the tensions in Marxist theory. They, like others on the New Left, have failed to produce a cohesive critical theory of society. As Alvin Gouldner points out: "Lacking the time or the impulse to develop their own theories, the Radicals' need of a theory is today satisfied by a hastily gulped, vulgar Marxism."[12]

This book is laid out to argue that there is in the corpus of Mills's work a comprehensive model which can not only replace functionalism but also provide the basis for "praxis" radical sociologists seek. After a biographical chapter, chapter three traces the intellectual influences on Mills in light of their relationship to his model.

Since the model in *Character and Social Structure* is so crucial to my analysis, chapter four deals exclusively with this work. Chapters five through eight represent a chronological presentation of Mills's writings as they pertain to the model. Chapter five focuses upon the writings of the young Mills, who while still a graduate student published widely in the area of the sociology of knowledge. Stratification became his major interest once he left graduate school, and chapter six analyzes Mills's articles written in the 1940's which deal with stratification as well as *The New Men of Power* (1948) and *White Collar* (1951). *The Power Elite* (1956), Mills's most famous and controversial work, is also wedded to his views on stratification; but because it was written after Mills completed his model, a separate chapter, chapter seven, is devoted to it. The major part of chapter eight deals with *The Sociological Imagination.* And, as I have stated, Mills here refined his model. The model is also implicit in Mills's last published book, *The Marxists,* and this work, too, will be taken up in chapter eight. Chapter nine is an evaluation or more appropriately a reevaluation of what constitutes Mills's rightful place in contemporary sociological theory. Specifically, I will focus upon Mills's relationship to what is now known as "radical sociology" and show how Mills's model offers the structural perspective that radical sociologists are searching for.

In short, nothing less than a reinterpretation of the judgment of C. Wright Mills as an unsystematic thinker will be attempted. By focusing upon Mills's lifelong attempt to synthesize pragmatism and Weberian sociology and his eventual completion of this task in the form of an historically based social-psychological working model of a social system, I intend to show that C. Wright Mills made an extremely valuable contribution to the systematic understanding of the interrelationship of man and society and their intersection in history.

2

C. WRIGHT MILLS—A BIOGRAPHICAL SKETCH

C. Wright Mills was a man of boundless, restless, almost uncontrollable energy. A Wobbly, he was spawned out of a unique union of American pragmatism and Southwestern populism. A perfectionist spurred less by ambition than by an intense belief in the efficacy of ideas, he wrote eleven books and over two hundred articles before he finally pushed himself so hard that he died spent at the age of forty-five. Few men have left so large an intellectual legacy, and fewer still were as controversial and misunderstood. While the reasons for the controversy and misunderstanding are many and varied, most are reducible to a common denominator—people see what they want to see, hear what they want to hear. And unfortunately this is true even in the academic world, where a professed search for truth so often gives way to vested intellectual interests. C. Wright Mills saw a different America than his academic peers, and he paid the price for his heterodoxy. While others, pale by comparison to his massive intellect, reaped the rewards of their profession (government grants, travel funds, secretarial help, distinguished chairs, etc.), Mills was forced to live off advances of books not yet written, and he died nine thousand dollars in debt—his wife having to borrow money from her father to bury him.[1]

Only now, more than a decade after his death, is Mills beginning to get the recognition he deserves. And even this is being given for the most part by younger, more radical, sociologists—those who have embraced Mills more for his heroics and colorful exploits than for his sociological writings.

It is high time then for the misunderstandings to be cleared up—to pare away the myth and define Mills's place in twentieth-century American sociology. And because Mills's life was so intertwined with his writings, the logical place to begin is with Mills the man.

C. Wright Mills was born in Waco, Texas, on August 28, 1916, the second child and only son of middle-class Irish and English Catholic parents. He grew up in Sherman, Fort Worth, and Dallas, attending both parochial and public schools. By his own admission he was shy and introspective, and the fact that his family moved eight times before he completed high school added to the loneliness felt by the young Mills. Slow to make friends, he inevitably had to move and leave those few he found. Like so many other boys in similar predicaments, he turned to adults for attention: his mother (his father, Charles Mills, travelled a great deal and was not as important an influence as was Mrs. Frances Mills),[2] teachers, a parish priest, and, later, college professors. While psychoanalysts might have a field day tracing the oedipal implications of growing up dominated by a mother and older sister, Mills himself always felt that his mother's influence was a healthy one, that the feminine values she instilled in him enhanced his sensitivity.

At an early age it was plain that there was something different about little Charlie Mills. (He dropped the Charles while in college and thereafter used the initial C and his middle name, Wright.) He would stand up to adults, teachers, and principals when he thought he was right, and unlike most small children, he refused to back down.[3] An early example of this stubbornness or as his mother called it, "his unbeatable will" occurred when Mills was only seven years old. His family had moved into a new neighborhood, and Mills was put back a grade in school. He refused to attend school until he was placed in his right grade with boys his own age and size. He would not budge on the matter, and the principal of the parochial school finally gave in and young Charles triumphantly returned to class.

The boy also possessed a tenacious faith in his own abilities, something that was to stay with him all his life. When asked by his family why he had not graduated at the top of his high school class (his grades were average) Mills replied, "I didn't want to." Given his later intellectual achievements, it seems likely that this was truly the reason.

Mills's elementary and high school years were basically unhappy ones. Loneliness and introspection characterized him. What support he received came exclusively from adults. Years later he would write: "I have never known what others call 'fraternity' with any group . . . neither academic nor political. With a few individuals, yes, but with small groups, no."[4]

High school on the whole, though, was a happier time than elementary school. Here Mills first developed the sense of craftsmanship that would become so important a part of his life. Possessing a genuine gift for carpentry, he would spend hours building his own sailboat. This interest in woodworking soon broadened to include architecture, and the young Mills even helped design his parents' home in Dallas. Due to his concern for architecture and the influence of a high school teacher, Mills transferred to Dallas Technical High School, graduating in 1934. (Daniel Smoot, the ultraconservative ex-FBI man, author of *The Dan Smoot Report,* was a classmate of his.)

That fall, Mills entered Texas A&M—in his father's words, "to make a man of" the shy, withdrawn youngster. He spent one year at this rural military school, a year that he always considered one of the most miserable of his life. He was accused of needlessly injuring another boy during a wrestling match, and his punishment was that no one was to speak to him. Again cut off from those his own age, he retreated to a previous pattern and sought the attention of adults. While none of his classmates spoke to him, and he in turn spoke to no one, he at least could impress his professors. But this was only a temporary solution at best, and the following fall Mills transferred to the University of Texas at Austin. There, in a different environment, he made two or three friends, almost an army in comparison with his Texas A&M experience. He later believed that these friendships were all that kept him from having a nervous breakdown.

Mills was now in a much friendlier milieu, and he slowly began to overcome his shyness. Wright found too that he could easily excel intellectually. A metamorphosis began to take place, and the withdrawn youngster slowly became outgoing. A whole new world opened up to him, a world of books, music, theater. And the boy who had until then heard only country and western music and had never seen a play, finally began to fit into the world of the college intellectual. He married Freya Smith in his junior year. In his senior year he was elected to Phi Beta Kappa and was made president of Alpha Kappa Delta, the national honor society in sociology.

It was here, too, at Texas that Mills was exposed to philosophical and social influences that would stay with him throughout his life. From Professor George Gentry, who had studied under George Herbert Mead, Mills learned about the pragmatists, those American philosophers who placed such faith in reason as a guide to freedom. From Clarence Ayers, a former assistant of Thorstein Veblen, he learned about "vested interests" and the role of the "leisure class" in American society.

The years at Texas were a period of awakening. New ideas began to come alive for him. It was a time to grow, and, as is often the case, a time to rebel. C. Wright Mills was perfectly suited for this role. He played the intellectual rebel to the hilt, from the stack of books he carried to the fur hats and outlandish clothes he purposely wore. Unlike most college students of the depression-ridden America of the late thirties, Mills never outgrew this role. His early years of isolation had left their mark, and Mills could maintain himself against any pressure that would try to limit his personal autonomy. Years later he described himself in these words:

I am a Wobbly. But do you know what a Wobbly is? It's a kind of spiritual condition . . . Wobbly is not only a man who takes orders from himself. He's also a man who's often in the situation where there are no regulations to fall back upon, which he hasn't made up himself. He doesn't like bosses, capitalistic or communistic, they're all the same to him. He wants to be, and he wants everyone else to be, his own boss at all times under all conditions and for any purposes they may want to follow up. This kind of spiritual condition, and only this is Wobbly freedom.[5]

He never relinquished the idealistic belief that ideas really do count, that they can produce change if enough people are just made aware of them. Intellectualism had been his salvation, carrying him from the obscurity of a small Texas town to celebrity status in the 1950's, and Mills reasoned that if ideas produced so much change in his life, they could do so for others, and his struggles to get other intellectuals to see this became a major theme in his life and in his writings.

The years he spent at the University of Texas were happy years, quite likely the first in his life. Perhaps this is why he chose to be an academic. Academia meant staying in the womb, a refusal to grow up. When he was in his forties he wrote: "I hope I have not grown up. The whole notion of growing up is pernicious, and I am against it. To grow up means merely to lose the intellectual curiosity so many children and so few adults seem to have . . ."[6]

Mills stayed to take a master's degree in philosophy at Texas, and the following year (1939) decided to go to the University of Wisconsin and "compete with the big boys." Unable to get an assistantship in philosophy, he accepted one in sociology. Although sociology was his second choice, Mills quickly distinguished himself at Wisconsin. He immediately came under the influence of Hans Gerth, a brilliant young scholar who had fled Nazi Germany. Gerth recognized Mills's potential and from the first accepted the young man as an equal. The two began, at Wisconsin, the only real intellectual collaboration Mills ever engaged in.[7]

Mills was quickly acknowledged to be the fair-haired boy of the sociology department, the most brilliant graduate student at Wisconsin. While there he began his scholarly career by publishing a number of articles in what was then a new area in American sociology, the sociology of knowledge. These articles, written originally as term papers, were highly technical and geared to a select audience of professional sociologists. In them, Mills combined American pragmatism with the writings of Karl Mannheim, who had been a teacher of Hans Gerth. One article, "The Professional Ideology of Social Pathologists," published in 1943 but written a few years before, is seminal

for an understanding of Mills's later thinking. In this now classic essay
Mills analyzed sociologists themselves. He scorned those who wrote in
the field of social problems for tacitly sanctioning the norms of American
society, for calling for socialization as a solution for all ills. Mills was one
of the earliest American sociologists to deal with the notion of ideology in
sociology. His writings raised the question of how "value-free" and
"objective" a discipline sociology was. This at a time when American
sociology was just beginning to establish itself as an academic discipline by
professing itself as characterized by these criteria. The article is considered
by many young sociologists to have signaled the beginnings of "radical
sociology," that branch of contemporary sociology which takes as given
the impossibility of "value-freedom" and "objectivity" in the social
sciences. For Mills, "The Professional Ideology of Social Pathologists"
represented an opening thrust into one of the major areas he would concern himself with from then on, the nature of sociology and the role of
power in American society. As Mills began to mature as a scholar, these
two areas became more and more entwined, and he came to hold that the
accumulation and dissemination of knowledge take place within a political
context. The sociologist, the intellectual, was ultimately working in the
political arena. One was either a political intellectual or an intellectual
eunuch. In Mills's thinking, there was no middle ground. This line of
reasoning took on a definite form when World War II broke out. Mills's
pursuit of truth up to then had been purely academic. The war changed
all that, and Mills, who had completed his Ph.D. in 1942 and taken a
teaching position at the University of Maryland, became a political radical.
In his own words:

I was an adolescent during the "thirties": at the midpoint of that decade,
I was 19. I don't know how typical I am of that "generation" in one very
important respect: I did not personally experience the "thirties." At that
time, I just didn't get its mood. I've got that only later and indirectly. Only
with the onset of World War II did I become radically aware of public
affairs, or aware in any way. I was, I suppose, too young; I was in an out-
lying region—Texas; I was not really alert to any sort of politics—studying
philosophy, especially logic, at the time. And above all, it happened that
during the "thirties" I was reading the literature of the "twenties."
    I sometimes think that during the "thirties" I was living in the "twenties,"
and that during the early "forties" I was living in the "thirties."[8]

Although opposed to the war, Mills at first took no open moral stance.
Only when the war touched him personally via the draft did he react
overtly. If drafted he would have had to fight in a war he did not believe
in, while refusal meant a jail term. Either way, his will, his reason, meant

little when faced with what he would later call "the blind drift of history." Before he could make a decision one was made for him. He was rejected by the army because of hypertension. The essential arbitrariness of the situation compounded his frustration, and rather than simply considering himself lucky, he became radicalized. The conflict between society and the individual he would so eloquently document was now rooted in his own experience, and his writings began to take on the political tone he would become famous for. From then on he was a political intellectual, a man who used his mind and sensibilities to make fate less unjust. An intellectual had to be his own man, a radical unencumbered by such artificial labels as nationalism and patriotism. Above all else the intellectual demanded that reason and cultivated sensibility have a role in human affairs. The war, in Mills's eyes, was unreasonable. To him there was little difference between Hitler's Germany and Roosevelt's America. He began to attack both, his position different from most radical critics of the time, critics who were essentially Marxist. Too young to have had the contact with Marxism (as had most radicals in the 1930's), Mills came to radicalism with an almost pure ideology. (He did not read Marx until the mid-1950's, and, as was his habit, he read all of Marx that was available in English translation. Mills never learned to read German.) As early as 1942, Mills was arguing that economic power is always subordinate to legal and social regulations. The United States, to him, was essentially a political economy. Business and government were becoming intertwined.[9] It was only a short step to the inclusion of the military. Mills took this step in another 1942 article, a review of Franz Neumann's *Behemoth: The Structure and Practice of National Socialism.* Here Mills focuses upon Neumann's position that four strategic elites dominated Nazi Germany: the monopoly capitalists, the Nazi party, the state bureaucracy, and the armed forces. Mills likened Nazi Germany to America. According to him, the National Association of Manufacturers (NAM) was similar to the German *Spitzenverbände,* whose collusion with the German state and army had been a major cause of World War II. In this review, Mills generally accepts the theory that fascism is linked to a monopoly capitalism infused with the state and implemented by the army. This is the genesis of Mills's famous power elite theory of a tripartite ruling group in America: those who hold the top positions in the political, economic, and military orders.

Although he did not believe that America was a fascist state, the war showed him the awful totalitarian potential of the United States. He never ceased to be a vocal critic of the war, one of the few intellectuals who consistently remained so. When others condemned John L. Lewis and the United Coal Miners' defiance of the War Labor Board in 1943, Mills defended

Lewis in an article in *The New Republic*. When he first met a famous American philosopher, Mills stated that he was "astounded that a man who considered himself as any sort of an intellectual could have participated in the war effort."

At the war's end, Mills was convinced that the United States was becoming a permanent war economy. He called upon the only two agents he saw as capable of stopping this trend, proposing an alliance of labor and intellectuals, the power and the intellect as he liked to call it.

Mills had come to New York in 1945 to teach at Columbia University and to head the labor research division of its Bureau of Applied Social Research. By 1946, he stopped writing for such leftist journals as *The New Leader, The New Republic*, and *Partisan Review* and almost completely dissociated himself from his at best marginal position in New York radical intellectual circles. Mills's concern in this period was with labor. In the late 1940's he published almost exclusively in *Labor and Nation*, an independent trade union periodical edited by J. B. Hardman. Most of the articles Mills wrote as an associate editor of the journal were related to the analysis of labor leaders the Bureau of Applied Research had undertaken for the Inter-Union Institute.

Mills's efforts in the late 1940's did not work out as well as he hoped; as he became more knowledgeable about the internal workings of labor, he, like so many others, began to lose faith in labor's ability to produce radical change in American society. By the 1950's Mills dismissed the trade union movement as an extension of the power elite.

Mills was also becoming thoroughly angered at the intellectuals. Given his views about labor, they now represented the only hope for stopping the drift toward a garrison state, and in his eyes they had to express themselves by a political (which to Mills meant radical) stance. He first articulated this anger in an early article, "The Powerless People: The Role of the Intellectual in Society" (1944).[10] Here Mills chastised his fellow intellectuals for being detached spectators. By adopting the pose of waiting for more knowledge before acting they manifested a political failure of nerve that gave way to a tragic sense of life.

As the 1940's came to an end Mills became angrier and angrier at his fellow intellectuals. The war years had been a period of broad disenchantment for many of America's intellectuals and radicals. Faced with the realities of the bureaucratization of American society and the totalitarianism of Soviet Russia, most political intellectuals moved away from Marxism as a viable alternative for change and toward an ideological vacuum. The times were characterized by a retreat from political stances to cultural ones. Marxism and its doctrine of a class struggle had failed America's radicals. Capitalism was not the enemy, bureaucracy was. Stalinist Russia was even worse than the United States. One had little choice between the East and West, and if one did choose the West, as Dwight MacDonald did in his famous 1952 Mount Holyoke debate with Norman Mailer, one made the choice with little enthusiasm. This was the beginning of the decline of radicalism so obvious in the United States of the 1950's, a decline that would produce an almost orgiastic celebration of America in the "end of ideology" movement of the late 1950's and early 1960's.

Mills, never having been a Marxist and only tangentially exposed to Marxist intellectual circles, was not disillusioned, and he held steadfast to his own particular brand of radicalism. His background of isolation led him to consider the rampant intellectual cult of alienation as a form of adolescent dilettantism and self-pity. Mills had little use for such indulgences. There was too much to do. What disillusionment Mills experienced was solely of a personal nature. His first marriage had broken up, and he felt bad that he had not been awarded custody of his daughter, Pamela.[11] In 1947 Ruth Harper, who had been a statistician at the Bureau of Applied Social Research, became the second Mrs. Mills.

With the onset of the 1950's Mills began to come into his own, both as a scholar and a celebrity. *White Collar* (1951), his second book (Mills had published *The New Men of Power* in 1948) was an overwhelming critical and commercial success. *White Collar* was almost universally hailed as a superb social-psychological study of how the bureaucratization of the economy shaped the personalities of individuals, covering much the same ground mined by David Riesman and William H. White, Jr.

Character and Social Structure, coauthored with Hans Gerth, his friend and former teacher at Wisconsin, followed in 1953.

Of importance, too, in terms of the direction in which Mills was moving, were two articles published in 1953 and 1954: "Two Styles of Social Science Research" and "IBM Plus Reality Plus Humanism = Sociology." Both caused quite a stir among sociologists. In these two articles Mills postulated the existence of two modes of inquiry in contemporary social science: the macroscopic and the microscopic. These in turn brought about two styles of craftsmanship. The macroscopic tradition claimed classical thinkers such as Max Weber, Karl Mannheim, Georg Simmel, and Karl Marx. Macroscopic sociologists dealt with such concepts as social structures, general types of historical phenomena, interconnecting institutional orders, and the relations of prevailing types produced in any given society. The molecularists, on the other hand, were characterized by small-scale problems and statistical models of verification. Mills was extremely sarcastic in his description of microscopic sociology, dismissing it as little more than nose counting.

Mills was now beginning to attack sociologists at the jugular. Microscopic sociologists constituted the overwhelming majority of American sociologists, and it is an understatement to say that Mills's description of them and their work was less than kind. Although Mills himself had done this type of research, he now demeaned it. He reasoned that the failure of labor had left intellectuals as the last hope for American society. Sociologists, those intellectuals he knew best, were wasting their potential on insignificant work. In his next book, *The Power Elite* (1956), Mills tried to show them what "grown men" should concern themselves with. *The Power Elite* is Mills's most controversial work and the one that he is best known for. The book is interesting not only for its thesis that a power elite ruled America, but for the reactions it created. Mills was attacked from both the academic right and left. Pluralists and Marxists alike tried to dismiss Mills's argument. What support he did receive, interestingly enough, came mostly from nonacademics.

Mills himself was generally pleased with the reaction to *The Power Elite*. Controversy upped sales, and he was interested in reaching as large an audience as possible. Mills had enjoyed writing the book even though it went through seven drafts, and he was delighted by the dispute surrounding it. Unfortunately, this ability to genuinely enjoy himself is something that most accounts of Mills overlook. A former assistant of his told me that Mills had put a few double entendres in *The Power Elite* and had laughed uproariously when people caught the double meaning. The journalist Dan Wakefield, a former student and friend of Mills, writes of this side of Mills:

He told me about attending a party of Columbia graduate students in sociology. . . .
"I simply sat in a chair in a corner," he said, and one by one these guys would come up to me, sort of like approaching the pariah—curiosity stuff. They were working on their Ph.d's you see, and after they'd introduced themselves I'd ask, 'What are you working on?' It would always be something like 'The Impact of Work-Play Relationships Among Lower Income Families on the South Side of the Block on 112th Street Between Amsterdam and Broadway.' And then I would ask—" Mills paused, leaned forward, and in his most contemptuous voice boomed: "Why?"[12]

There was, of course, that other side to Mills—the aggressive, gruff, irascible side that most people saw. Mills, wanting to accomplish so much, could be short with those who were not seen as allies.

With the publication of *The Power Elite*, C. Wright Mills became even more of a celebrity—the "Texas Trotsky," someone dubbed him. A careful reading of *The Power Elite* would have revealed its essentially anti-Marxist approach, but most critics refused to read it carefully, some even preferring to treat the book as what would later come to be called a "happening."

The media were now beginning to be interested in Mills. Given the usual run-of-the-mill academician, Mills was a godsend. Stories were written about him, photos were shown of him riding to his classes at Columbia University on a BMW motorcycle, complete with goggles, boots, and leather jacket. His feuds with his colleagues became common knowledge and then passed beyond the realm of truth to legend. A particularly persistent myth has it that Mills, because of his disagreements with his colleagues at Columbia, was not permitted to teach graduate students. The truth is that Mills, after teaching in the graduate school at Columbia for a short time, decided it was too time-consuming and that nothing of any consequence was accomplished at any of the meetings of the graduate faculty. Mills thereupon asked the chairman, Robert Merton, if he could teach full-time in the undergraduate college. Merton agreed, and Mills never regretted the decision. Another equally persistent myth is that because of the radical political stances Mills took throughout his career he was never promoted to full professor at Columbia.[13] Mills was promoted to full professor in 1956, at a younger age than most academics in prestigious universities.

What is not a myth, though, was the vicious critical attacks Mills's later works were subjected to. *The Power Elite*, in particular, was judged by Mills's academic peers as having no scholarly value. Mills was compensated however, by the popular success of *The Power Elite*, a work which still sells thousands of copies a year.

Mills followed *The Power Elite* with a paperback book, *The Causes of World War III* (1958). This pamphlet, as Mills called it, sold in the hundreds of thousands, a figure unheard of at the time for a work by a sociologist. Here Mills argued that the power elite in America and its Soviet counterpart were leading the two nations to a total and absurd war. Mills tried to do something to stop this trend, speaking out as a man who considered himself sane in an insane world. Writing as a popularist, he still harbored the belief from his college days that if enough people could hear the truth they might take action. Paperback publishing was opening up a new world for the intellectual, and Mills found it hard to believe that his fellow intellectuals refused to take advantage of the possibilities of reaching a mass audience. By continuing to write in what Malcolm Cowley once dubbed "socspeak" and publishing in esoteric journals, sociologists were supporting the drift toward America's becoming a permanent war economy.

Mills was particularly proud of a section in *The Causes of World War III* entitled "A Pagan Sermon to the Christian Clergy." In this essay, later reprinted in *The Nation*, he expressed disbelief that the clergy had not openly condemned the military definition of reality so characteristic of the 1950's.

Most of his anger, though, was still directed at his academic cohorts. In 1959, *The Sociological Imagination* was published. The work broke with the genteel tradition of academia, launching a personal attack on leading members of the sociological profession and the schools of thought associated with them. Although not widely read outside the academic world, *The Sociological Imagination* quickly became a classic in sociology and a rallying point for those who disagreed with establishment sociology. In it Mills restates the position of the pragmatists, the notion that the mind is not a passive spectator in the knowing process—that knowledge is intrinsically related to activity. However, while the pragmatists took for granted that reason led to freedom, Mills argued that in the modern era this was simply not so. The individual's path to freedom lay in becoming aware of the structural constraints which determined his existence, and intervening to do something about them. Sociology should point out just what these constraints were. Reason and freedom should be "value-judgments" in all research. This openly interventionist position was untenable to most sociologists, who argued that the development of science was dependent on the institutionalization of objectivity. Sociologists, they argued, must concern themselves with that which is and never what ought to be.

Mills, although he still enjoyed a good fight, did not engage in the debate that raged around *The Sociological Imagination*—at least not to the degree he had with *The Power Elite*.[14] He had more important things to do. In January of 1960, Mills had visited Mexico, and out of his meetings and discussions with Latin American intellectuals had become extremely interested in Cuba. He returned to the United States in April of 1960 with tentative plans to write about Castro's revolution. The book had to be postponed for a while, though: Mills, upon arriving home, found an invitation from the Soviet-American Friendship Society to visit Russia. He jumped at the chance. Mills's third wife, Yaroslava Surmach Mills (he had divorced his second wife in 1957) was about to give birth and could not travel, so Mills went alone. He spent three weeks touring and conducting interviews with Russians. He came home exhausted, but with notebooks filled with information for a book he had long planned, now tentatively entitled *Tovarich: Contacting the Enemy*. In this work Mills wanted to tell what it meant to be a political intellectual in American society and how he had become one. It was the closest he ever came to writing an autobiography. Mills planned to send mimeographed manuscripts to Russian intellectuals, and hoped one would answer back, explaining the position of the Soviet intellectual. He never got beyond a first draft of this work. When he returned to the United States, Cuba became more and more his preoccupation. Here was an indigenous revolution created and successfully completed by intellectuals. What he had been saying in theory was possible in practice. The intellectual could be the agent for historical change. Mills rushed off to Cuba, taped interviews with Fidel Castro and other leaders, and came back to write *Listen, Yankee* (1960) in six weeks. The book, an attempt to explain the Cuban Revolution through the eyes of the Cuban revolutionary, evoked even more criticism from the academic community than had *The Power Elite* or *The Causes of World War III*. But the nearly half a million copies sold, and the thousands of letters of praise and, more important, questions about what could be done received from readers more than made up for the scholarly vitriol *Listen, Yankee* attracted. Mills was convinced he was on the right track. At last he was beginning to reach a large enough audience to offset the power elite. If only people could be made more aware. A new career was dawning. He would be the one who would make them aware, dispel the false consciousness that enveloped American society. Other intellectuals, he hoped, would join in too. But Mills never got the chance to carry out his plans. An earlier heart attack in Denmark, which had gone undiagnosed, along with the strain of his work-load, proved too great. He had a second heart attack. Under doctor's orders, he began to slow down. A proposed debate on national television with A. A. Berle, Jr. on United States Latin American policy had to be postponed and eventually cancelled. Other pressures began to mount. Mills, who had always lived on advances for his books (Columbia University paid exceedingly low wages), found himself in financial trouble. A Cuban exile who claimed that Mills had libelled him in *Listen, Yankee* filed suit. *Listen, Yankee*, a paperback, brought in royalties of only a few cents a copy, and most of this Mills had already spent to finance research for future books.

Mills's doctor advised him to forget about his problems, to leave the country, travel about, go camping, perhaps even to visit Russia again. The young doctor had read of recent Russian breakthroughs in the treatment of heart disease and thought it might be worthwhile for Mills to see if the Russians could help his condition.

Mills, his wife, his newborn son, his daughter Katie by his second marriage, and Saul Landau, acting as a research assistant, took off for Europe. There the Mills entourage travelled from campsite to campsite in a Volkswagen bus until they eventually reached the Russian border.

Once there they found they could only enter by invitation. After minor skirmishes with bureaucratic red tape, Mills received the necessary invitation, and they entered Russia. Unfortunately, after a routine medical inspection, it was suspected that Mills's son, Niki, had dysentery, and the child and his mother were sent to a Russian hospital. Mills stayed in a Russian hotel with his daughter and Landau. There, waiting for the release of his wife and son, he began to realize that unlike the United States, where one could at least choose doctors, once entering a Russian hospital he would be completely under the authority of physicians. When Yaroslava and Niki were finally released, Mills denounced what he called "a dictatorship of doctors" and told of his decision to leave Russia. Using money from the royalties of the Russian edition of *The Power Elite,* he purchased tickets for a ship bound for England.

Mills rested in England, trying to gain back the strength that had been his trademark. His enthusiasm was as high as ever. He even designed a black suit (he designed all of his clothes) which he jokingly called his "preacher's suit." Having already given his "Pagan Sermon to a Christian Clergy," he would now preach to the masses.

In that summer of 1961, Mills was offered an ideal situation, one which would never have been open to him in the United States. As chairman of the sociology department at the new University of Sussex at Brighton, he would not have to teach, and would have ample time to write. His wife, aware of the tensions awaiting him when they returned home, urged him to accept the offer. Mills considered it and almost accepted, but his experiences, his radicalism, were too American to permit him to do so. He simply told his wife: "These are just not my people; their problems are not my problems."

The Mills party made plans to visit the novelist Harvey Swados, one of Mills's oldest and closest friends, at Swados's villa in the south of France. On the way, Mills stopped at Paris, meeting with Jean Paul Sartre and Simone de Beauvoir.

Inevitably Cuba came up in the conversation. Mills was more optimistic about Cuba's chances for survival than was Sartre, hoping that Castro would somehow manage to preserve what was good about the Cuban Revolution.[15] But Mills was having his doubts; he was genuinely struggling with his feelings toward Cuba when he arrived at Swados's villa. Swados held out little hope for democratization in Cuba and argued his position persuasively. Castro had personally promised Mills that he would never embrace communism, and now had. So much of Mills's long-time belief that intellectuals could make a difference was tied up with Castro's struggles that he could not help feeling betrayed. Mills left France for America "torn between defending *Listen, Yankee* as a good and honest book and acknowledging publicly for the first time in his life that he had been terribly wrong."[16]

Mills and family arrived home on January 27, 1962. Believing that he had regained his strength, Mills quickly began to work. It soon became obvious that he had not recovered, and all he was able to do was put the finishing touches on *The Marxists* (1962).

C. Wright Mills died peacefully in his sleep on March 20, 1962. Left unfinished were *Tovarich; The Cultural Apparatus,* a tentatively titled study of intellectuals; a work on the New Left; and what was to have been Mills's *magnum opus, Comparative Sociology,* a work of at least five volumes, in which Mills would analyze the social structures of different countries[17] (living in each for a while, doing "on the spot sociology" as he called it).

Mills was buried in the black "preacher's suit" he had never gotten to wear, his final views on Cuba buried with him. The booming, so often lonely voice of American radicalism was stilled.

3

INFLUENCES ON MILLS

There is a model implicit in the writings of C. Wright Mills—a model that may prove to be an alternative to structure-functional and conflict models. In this chapter I examine intellectual influences upon Mills, those schools of thought and representative thinkers that played a major role in the formation of Mills's model. They are, in order of Mills's exposure to them, pragmatism, Weberian sociology, neo-Freudianism, and Marxism. In terms of their relative importance for Mills's intellectual development, pragmatism and Weberian sociology rank as primary influences, while neo-Freudianism and Marxism, to which Mills was exposed quite late in life, are of secondary importance.

Pragmatism, as exemplified by the social behaviorism of George Herbert Mead, provided the underpinnings for Mills's theory of the development of the self. Drawing upon neo-Freudian interpretations, Mills amplified Mead's notion of the social definition of personality formation to include a perspective which took into account the sociological concept of social structure. In order to provide the necessary bridge to jump from personality to society, Mills borrowed Max Weber's concept of "social relationship." From Karl Mannheim came the notion of how societies are integrated. As for Karl Marx, he was more of a general influence and less important to Mills than Mead, Weber, and Mannheim were. Mills essentially carried on the dialogue that Weber and Mannheim had engaged in with Marx, and he tried to relate what he considered to be Marxist determinism to the subjective, volitional side of human life.

PRAGMATISM

Mills openly acknowledges his debt to Mead in *Character and Social Structure*, stating a desire to combine Mead with Freud in order to arrive at a convergence of the social and psychological bases of personality. Actually, however, Freud's specific contribution to Mills's theory of personality formation is quite meager. As Don Martindale observes:

In their conception of character they [Gerth and Mills] have actually taken precious little from Freud. Of such conceptions as the unconscious, conscious, censor, id, superego, ego, repression, sublimation, auto-eroticism, Oedipus Complex, Electra Complex, dream symbolism, they make practically no use. Rather, the materials formed by social roles into character are conceived originally to break down into sensation, feeling, and impulse, which by language are transformed into perception, emotion, and purpose. Freud actually receives little more than lip service.[1]

While Freud as a specific influence can be dismissed, the neo-Freudians, Fromm, Horney, and particularly Sullivan, are a different matter. After a brief summary of Mead, the neo-Freudian influences upon Mills will be taken up. But first, Mead.

George Herbert Mead

For Mead, "mind is the presence in behavior of significant symbols."[2] The mind is not a physical substance with a specific location in the brain. It is rather the functioning of significant symbols. These symbols arise only in the social process. Therefore, instead of beginning with the mind of the individual and working outward to a society, Mead reverses the usual procedure and through the social process of communication works inward to the individual via the vocal gesture. Mind is a social concept. Thought proceeds through an individual's assuming other people's roles. He then modifies and controls his own behavior in terms of such role taking. Thinking occurs through the internalized conversation of gestures and attitudes, the individual taking both an objective and a subjective stance. This conception of gesture is extremely important in Mead's analytical scheme because it modifies Wundt's notion of the gesture, as Wundt has previously modified Darwin's. According to Mead, the term *gesture* is identified with the beginnings of social acts which are in turn stimuli for the response of other forms. Darwin was originally interested in gestures because they expressed emotions, and he dealt with them largely as if this were their only function in the animals under study. To Darwin, the gestures of a dog expressed the joy with which it accompanied its master. In Mead's words:

It was easy for Wundt to show that this was not a legitimate point of
attack on the problem of these gestures. They did not at bottom serve the
function of expression of the emotions; that was not the reason why they
were stimuli, but rather because they were parts of complex acts in which
different forms were involved. They became the tools through which the
other forms responded. When they did give rise to a certain response, they
were themselves changed in response to the change which took place in the
other form.[3]

To this Mead adds that on the human level the gesture means the idea
behind it. When it arouses that idea in the other individual a significant
symbol is present. Vocal gestures are those gestures which are capable of
becoming significant symbols, in this manner transforming the biological
individual into a mind. No other gesture or symbol is as successful in
affecting the individual while simultaneously affecting others. Speech is of
primary importance because it alone stimulates the speaker and the hearer
in the same manner. This mechanism is found only in human society.
According to Mead, the vocal gesture provides the medium of social
organization in society.

Language makes the appearance of self possible. The mechanisms of
communication, symbols, language, and role taking result in the social
conception of mind. Man is a human being because he has the ability to
speak. Mead developed a new method which in turn produced a shift in
the basic assumptions underlying the nature and function of language.
Wundt had previously looked upon language as a means for the expression
of ideas. Mead and John Dewey, his friend and colleague, pioneered a
functional approach in which the nature of language is not the expression
of antecedent thought, but is essentially communication—the establishment
of cooperation in social activity—in which the self and the other are modified and regulated by the common act.

The self becomes social through the medium of language, which enables
the individual to role-play. Mead's famous example of the child at play
serves to illustrate how role playing comes about.

A child plays at being a mother, at being a teacher, at being a policeman;
that is, it is taking different roles, as we say. . . . When a child does assume a
role he has in himself the stimuli which call out that particular response or
group of responses. . . . Children get together to "play Indian." This means
that the child has a certain set of stimuli which call out in itself the responses
that they would call out in others and which answers to an Indian. In the
play period the child utilizes his own responses to these stimuli which he
makes use of in building a self. The response which he has a tendency to

make to these stimuli organizes them. He plays that he is, for instance, offering himself something, and he buys it; he gives a letter to himself and takes it away; he addresses himself as a policeman. He has a set of stimuli which call out in himself the sort of responses they call out in others. He takes this group of responses and organizes them into a certain whole. Such is the simplest form of being another to one's self. It involves a temporal situation. The child says something in one character and responds in another character, and then his responding in another character is a stimulus to himself in the first character, and so the conversation goes on. A certain organized structure arises in him and in his other which replies to it, and these carry on the conversation of gestures between themselves.[4]

In an organized game, the child must be ready to take the attitude of everyone else, and these different roles have a definite relationship to each other. For example, if a child participates in a game of baseball, he must be able to anticipate the responses of everyone else as they might affect his position. He has to know what everyone else might do in order for him to perform. In essence, he has to take into account all of the other roles.

The final crystallization of all these attitudes and responses is what Mead terms the "generalized other." This he defines as "the organized community or social group which gives to the individual his unity of self.... The attitude of the generalized other is the attitude of the whole group."[5] The generalized other is the universalization of the process of role taking. It is the general term that indicates all those who stand over against the self in his attitude of role taking with a cooperative activity.

Although the above synopsis of Mead's theory of the social development of the self cannot do justice to the breadth and insight of this distinguished social philosopher, it does provide a starting point for an analysis of Mills's conception of the self—for Mills's, too, is social.

A basic difference between the two is that for Mead, behavior is socially defined; for Mills, behavior is societally defined. This nuance is important because Mills was convinced that the pragmatists and even the social psychologists of his own time held an inadequate notion of what constituted a social structure. For Mills, societally defined behavior was institutionally defined behavior. The distinction becomes clearer if we single out specific concepts for analysis. Once such concept is impulse. For Mead, impulse implies a seeking of expression, with the implication being that the organism creates its own environment. Response is the reply to a stimulus which, in turn, terminates the chain of reactions which were set in motion by the impulsive act of the organism in selecting its stimulus. It is primarily the attempted completion or the satisfaction of the need of the organism. Impulse and response are subjective; stimulus is objective.

The response endows the environment with whatever meaning and structure it may have for the organism. Mills's position is somewhat different. For him impulses are directly linked to goals, which in turn sustain the roles the individual enacts. These roles are related to institutions, which comprise institutional orders and whose integration make up a social system.

Another basic point of departure relates to Mead's view of what constitutes the social environment. Mead envisions social structure as less organized than that of most sociologists and anthropologists, as something of a negotiated order—a viewpoint similar to that of Dewey.

Dewey, an important influence in his own right upon Mills, holds that "human nature" is limited only by the confines of "culture." The concept of culture presented in Dewey's *Freedom and Culture*, the concept to which Mills devotes a chapter in his doctoral dissertation, represents a modification of his earlier views concerning environmental influence upon the individual. In *Freedom and Culture*, as A. H. Somjee succinctly puts it, instead of "an overwhelming physical and institutionally bound social environment, Dewey substitutes the term 'culture' in order to indicate an amalgam of physical, biological, economic, political, religious, aesthetic, moral, scientific, and educational factors."[6]

Despite this modification, Dewey's "culture" still lacks a definite notion of social structure. This is precisely what Mills has in mind when he writes:

In place of social structure, many students would use the concept "culture"—one of the spongiest words in social science. The concept, "culture," is often more a loose reference to social milieu than an adequate notion of social structure.[7]

Mills's fundamental criticism of Mead is that Mead fails to develop an adequate notion of emotion and motives—a dynamic theory of the affective life of man. This failure is tied to Mead's inability to explain individual diversity and idiosyncratic behavior. While Mead shows that the self develops socially, that it mirrors the outside world, he never adequately deals with the internal discords of individuals. Mills attempts to go beyond Mead—to get at man the whole entity, both a biological organism and an historical creation. Freudian psychoanalytical theory, on the other hand, while explaining how man acts as a separate individual, leaves little room for an appreciation of the historical nature of the self. Freud's notion of personality is thereby too socially inflexible for Mills. How then could Mills solve this apparent dilemma? One way, which Mills takes, is to substitute a neo-Freudian framework for the rigid biological one offered by Freud. This preference for a neo-Freudian framework can be seen as early as 1945, when

Mills, replying to Paul Goodman's Reichian analysis of the political order, chooses an historical and sociological psychology. In this short piece, Mills is at his satirical best, reducing Goodman's views to "a gonad theory of revolution." Whether or not Mills adequately handles Goodman's subsequent rebuttal is not as important as the genesis of Mills's social psychology, particularly the role assigned to the Fromm-Horney sociological revision of orthodox Freudianism. According to Mills, any biological argument for the origins and perpetuation of a social structure is inadequate. In his words:

The capitalistic market cannot be derived from a study of the economic man, nor can the frustration which it causes be understood by examining man's *formal* biological equipment. Indeed, the specific impulses which sustain economic man are shaped by their operations on various types of markets. Impulses are given *content* only by the participation in given institutions. The content of frustration and the severe political direction which they may take are dependent upon the particular institutions men create.[8]

Mills is saying here that a man's innermost being is dependent upon the institutions in which he lives out his individual biography. Man is no mere biological creature simply reacting in order to satisfy physiological instincts. As Mills later observes: "From the rather abstract 'standpoint of society,' the question of impulse is: How can a person be produced who wants, or 'wills,' what is socially approved, demanded or premiumed."[9] Witness the similarity of outlook with the following statement from Erich Fromm's *Man for Himself:* "Society must tend to mold the character structure of its members in such a way that they will want to do what they have to do under existing circumstances."[10]

The sociologically imbued neo-Freudian conception of personality formation is instrumental for Mills's modification of Mead. Harry Stack Sullivan, especially in his use of the concept "significant other,"[11] is of particular importance. Mills relies heavily upon Sullivan for a modification of Mead's "generalized other." Concerning his differences with Mead, Mills states: "My conception of the generalized other differs from Mead's in one respect . . . I do not believe . . . that the generalized other incorporates 'the whole society,' but rather that it stands for selected societal segments."[12]

In Mills's scheme "significant others" are selected in terms of three institutionally defined principles: cumulative confirmations, selection by position and career, and the confirming use of the intimate other. The first of these, the principle of cumulative confirmation holds that the image of self a person possesses and prizes leads him to select and pay attention to those individuals who either confirm or enhance his self-image. By "selection by position and career" Mills means that the selection of significant others is limited to the institutional position of the individual and by the course of his career as he moves from one institutional position to another.

The third principle, the confirming use of the intimate other, comes into play only when the individual is thwarted in his search for significant others and reacts by choosing only, at most, a few significant others. These three principles of selection, while not exhausting all of the possibilities, are nevertheless the major ones and are intrinsically related to the manner in which institutions shape persons. Mills thus not only advocates an institutionally defined generalized other but also tries to explain the development of idiosyncratic behavior. The social relativity of the generalized other is only one phase of personality development. Any understanding of Mills's modification of Mead's social behaviorism rests with an analysis of Mills's notion of character structure. There are four components to Mills's character structure: organism, psychic structure, person, and character structure.[13] Organism refers to man as a biological creature. Yet to focus exclusively upon this facet of man's nature excludes the whole area of the "why" of man's conduct. Man as a member of the animal species is structurally limited, but this limitation does not determine him. Mills sums up his views on man as a biological organism in these words:

From the biological point of view, then, man as a species and men as individuals are seen as organisms (1) whose action is *structurally limited,* who are equipped with certain mechanical responses, and (2) who possess *undefined impulses,* which may be defined and specified by a wide range of social objects. What those objects may be is not determined by man as an organism.[14]

Psychic structure considers man as an integration of perception, emotion, and impulse. These three concepts which make up the psychic structure are rooted in the organism and can be affected by changes in the organism. However, if we are to really understand the psychic structure, the social milieu must be looked at, because organic features by themselves cannot explain an individual's psychic traits. Psychic traits are to be analyzed only in relation to socialization and social milieux of individuals. This, of course, does not mean that the organism is irrelevant to the formation of psychic traits, only that the organism takes on relevance only in terms of the meanings assigned to it by roles.

Undefined impulses are defined by socially acquired goals. Perceptions are conditioned by the organization of our sensations in accordance with accepted symbols and vocabularies. And emotions are defined via socially induced feeling states. In short, the development of the psychic structure—of impulses, perception, and emotion—always involves the social roles a person enacts.

Man as a player of roles is the key concept here. *Person,* as Mills uses the term, refers to just that. Through his experience, through his enactment of roles, the person incorporates certain objectives and more important values which shape not only his psychic structure but his character as well. Mills, by viewing man as a person, sought to understand conduct in terms of motive rather than explain it in terms of physiological constants in the organism.

Character structure is the most inclusive term for man as a whole entity, referring to the relatively stabilized integration of an organism's psychic structure. The psychic structure is in turn linked with the social roles of the person. Thus, on one hand, a character structure is anchored in the organism, and on the other is formed by the particular combination of social roles which the person incorporates from the myriad of the total roles available to him in his society. The uniqueness of any individual comes out of the specific organization of the component elements of the character structure.

This, then, is Mills's answer to Mead's inability to explain diversity among individuals. Basically, those differences found among men are attributable to the constitution of their organisms, to the specific role configurations incorporated in their person, and to the idiosyncratic integration of their perceptions, feelings, and will within a psychic structure. This idiosyncratic integration represents purposeful action on the part of the individual. In order to have a will an individual strives against something—man encounters resistance and in this manner orders his experience. Mills here adumbrates the social constructionist view of reality which would become popular in the 1960's. Witness the following passage:

The world we experience is in no small degree determined by our past experiences and future expectations, which form a "frame of reference" or "apperceptive mass," as it has been called. Because of this, man cannot be said to receive passively the world of sensations; he is an active determiner of what he perceives and experiences. For not only his sense organs but his apperceptive mass, with its social organization of feelings and impulses, is part of his perception. In this sense, man as a person constructs the world that he perceives, and this construction is a social act.[15]

An adequate portrayal of an individual's personality formation thus involves the analysis of four concepts within the institutional confines of a specific social structure, and most importantly as mediated by an active, volitional self.

Unable to accept Freud's biological orientation and ignorance of modern anthropology, Mills instead relies upon the neo-Freudian outlook that man, although he is limited by his biology, satisfies his needs in society. The individual has to be understood in relation to his society. The concept of role is the crucial link between the individual and his social structure. It is through man's ability to internalize roles that he becomes anchored to his society. Mills then turns to the writings of Max Weber to provide the necessary bridge between the amorphous notion of social structure found in the works of George Herbert Mead and the pragmatists and an adequate sociological conception of social structure.

WEBERIAN SOCIOLOGY

Out of the works of Max Weber and his intellectual heir, Karl Mannheim, Mills fashions the social structure part of his synthesis. Weber, like Mead, was interested in subjective actions; but, unlike Mead, he attempted to go beyond the individual by relating him to his social structure. This was accomplished by focusing upon social action as the basic unit of analysis. In Weber's own words, action is social if "by virtue of the subjective meaning attached to it by the acting individual (or individuals), . . . it takes account of the behavior of others and is thereby oriented in its course."[16] In order to go beyond social action and make the transition to social structure, Weber introduces the concept of "social relationship." This he defines as "the behavior of a plurality of actors in so far as, in its meaningful content, the action of each takes account of that of the others and is oriented in these terms."[17] Weber could then look at social structure as the probability that there will be some form of social action. Because Weber was a nominalist, the closest he could come to an objective social structure was one that dealt in objective probabilities. The Weberian social structure, then, does not divorce the individual and his action from the society, because it is conceived in terms of probable patterns of behavior. The concept of social relationship provides the bridge between individual actions and recurrent patterns of behavior. Social behavior is patterned because the individual expects that others will act in a certain way and adjusts his own behavior to these expectations accordingly. As long as there is a probability that his behavior will meet with expected reactions, and vice versa, a social structure exists. Social behavior thus develops and gives rise to patterned actions which are oriented by the actors to a belief in the existence of a legitimate order. An order exists when the subjective meaning of a social relationship is oriented to certain determinate maxims or rules, and there is the implicit recognition that they are binding on the individual.

Weber thus starts out with the idea of probability and shows how social conduct develops and gives rise to other actions which subsequently furnish the basis for political, economic, religious, and other organizations.[18]

In short, Weber begins with the individual act and through the concept of social relationship moves to the basic types of social behavior: associations, groups, institutions, and communities. His complex system of thought is a starting point for an analysis of Mills's views on social structure.

Gerth and Mills provided one of the first translations of Weber into English (1946) and stated their interpretation of Weber's concepts of social action, social relationship, and social structure, focusing on Weber's social-psychological orientation. Weber, in the words of his translators, conceives of man "as a composite of general characteristics derived from social institutions, the individual as an actor of social roles."[19] In *The Protestant Ethic and the Spirit of Capitalism,* Weber believes (according to Gerth and Mills) that modern capitalism when it began required a specific type of personality. This personality type, in turn, was formed psychologically by beliefs in a set of ideas that resulted in the development of those specific traits which were useful for a capitalistic system.

Gerth and Mills see Weber's translated works as dealing with the ideal personality types shaped by various social structures. Weber's studies of the Junker, the Indian Brahman, and the Chinese Literati fall into this category. Weber's social system is one which is made up of the interrelations of institutional orders. The concept role (or in Weber's terms, "calling" or "vocation," as presented in "Politics as a Vocation" and "Science as a Vocation") serves as the point of contact between personality structure, or character, and social structure. This social structure is interpreted by Gerth and Mills to be capitalism.

Weber contributes to Mills's social psychology by providing the means for going beyond the structureless social behaviorism of George Herbert Mead to an institutionally (via social relationship) defined social structure. What is lacking in Weber's sociology is an explanation of the manner in which institutions are interrelated or, to use Mills's term, "integrated." It is not enough to define the whole system as capitalism. There had to be a way to show how institutions are integrated to form various types of social structures. This is a necessity if Mills's synthesis is to be of any historical and cross-cultural value. The "way" is provided by Karl Mannheim. Before looking at Mannheim, something should be said about Weber's theory of social stratification, because it was almost wholly incorporated by Mills into his own scheme.

According to Mills, social stratification consists of four dimensions: occupation, class, status, and power. The dimensions of class, status, and power are taken directly from Weber's famous class, status, and party trichotomy of stratification. Occupation, the fourth concept, is also taken from Weber, who defines it as "the mode of specialization, specification, and combination of the functions of an individual so far as it constitutes for him the basis of a continual opportunity for income or for profit."[20] Although he alludes to the relationship of occupation to the problems of social stratification, Weber never develops it as fully as the other three.[21] This Weberian notion of stratification formed the basis for Hans Gerth's famous social stratification course given at the University of Wisconsin and is almost wholly incorporated into Mills's model.

In order to fully understand Mills we have to look at the indelible stamp Mannheim left upon his works.

KARL MANNHEIM

A great deal of the genesis of Mills's historically based sociology can be seen in Mannheim's *Man and Society in an Age of Reconstruction.* Mannheim, like Weber, is interested in an historical and social psychology, and calls for a discipline which would study the human mind in relation to changes in the social structure.

Mills's working model approach would echo, almost two decades later, these words of Karl Mannheim:

We are not yet accustomed to studying the human mind in relation to the changes in the social situation. For reasons which it is difficult to gauge, there is already a tendency in everyday life to concentrate almost exclusively either on the individual and his character or on the outside world, which by a typical simplification, is interpreted as a combination of a few vaguely apprehended factors. What we really need is a stubborn observation which never fails to perceive the social aspect of every psychological phenomenon and to interpret it in terms of a continual interaction between the individual and society. . . . Thus it will only be possible to look at history from a new angle when we can study the changes of the human mind in an historical setting, in close connection with the changes in the social structure.[22]

Mannheim, unlike Weber, focuses upon the internal workings of definite social structures. According to Mannheim, there are certain kinds of recurring special laws, special relationships of historical phases in a particular social setting; these, borrowing the term from John Stuart Mill, he calls "principia media." This is the closest he comes to defining how societies are integrated:

The *principia media* . . . are in the last analysis universal forces in a concrete setting as they become integrated out of the various factors at work in a given time, a particular combination of circumstances which may never be repeated. They are, then, on the one hand, reducible to the general principles which are contained in them . . . . But on the other hand, they are to be dealt with in their concrete settings as they confront us at a certain stage of development and must be observed within their individual patterns, with certain characteristic sub-principles which are peculiar to them alone.[23]

From this and other statements Mannheim makes, we can begin to see what he means by principia media. Essentially, principia media are those regularities and interconnections which define the pattern of a particular social milieu, or, to use Mills's terms, are "modes of integration" by which the institutions make up a social structure. The following passage from *Man and Society in an Age of Reconstruction* is offered to support this contention:

The most we can really see today is the interdependent modification of various *principia media* in the political, economic, technological, and psychological spheres. These modifications must be viewed as interdependent, i.e., the points must be discovered where changes in the political sphere, for instance, touch upon those in the economic, and where the changes in both these objective spheres bring about a subjective change in the form of a new psychological attitude.[24]

Mannheim's concept of principia media, although it does not solve the problem of how social structures are integrated and how this, in turn, produces psychological types, at least raises the question. Mills's answer to this question is an integral part of his model—his four principal modes of integration: correspondence, coincidence, coordination, and convergence. (These modes of integration will be more fully analyzed in the next chapter.)

MARXISM—A GENERAL INFLUENCE

So far, my concern has been with primary influences of pragmatism and German sociology upon Mills. I briefly noted that Marx was at best a secondary influence. This, of course, calls for further elaboration.

Perhaps Mills himself best sums up his relationship to Marxism in a reply to a reviewer of *The Power Elite* who hinted at sinister Marxist tendencies in Mills's work: Says Mills:

Let me say explicitly: I happen never to have been what is called "a

Marxist," but I believe Karl Marx one of the most astute students of society modern civilization has produced; his work is now essential equipment of any adequately trained social scientist as well as of any properly educated person. Those who say they hear Marxian echoes in my work are saying that I have trained myself well. That they do not intend this testifies to their own lack of proper education.[25]

A few years later, Mills stated basically the same thing in his critique of Marxism, *The Marxists.*

No one who does not come to grips with the ideas of Marxism can be an adequate social scientist; no one who believes that Marxism contains the last word can be one either. Is there any doubt about this after Max Weber, Thorstein Veblen, Karl Mannheim—to mention only three? We do now have ways—better than Marx's alone—of studying and understanding man, society, and history, but the work of these three is quite unimaginable without his work.[26]

If this is not proof enough to relegate Marx to a position of secondary importance in Mills's sociological thought, we have only to turn to some of Mills's works to verify this assertion.

In *White Collar,* for instance, the notion is developed that the "new middle classes" who do not own the means of production are not a Marxian "new proletariat." They do not fit into the classical Marxian class scheme, and indeed, Mills believed that the very existence of the "new middle class" contradicted the Marxian two-class model. *The Power Elite* is also notable for the great pains Mills went to in avoiding the Marxian concept of "ruling class." In a footnote on page 277 of *The Power Elite,* Mills says quite explicitly that *class* is an economic term and *rule* a political one. Mills painstakingly seeks to avoid the interpretation that an economic class rules politically. The term *ruling class* does not give enough autonomy to the political and leaves out the military entirely. Mills uses the term *power elite* to focus upon those in the higher echelons of political, economic, and military institutional orders. This rejection of an economically determined society for a picture of a social system composed of integrated institutional orders shows the pronounced influence of Weber, rather than Marx, upon Mills.

Along with his rejection of the term *ruling class,* Mills also goes against the Marxian grain by offering a portrait of an impotent mass. Indeed, the society pictured in *The Power Elite* is notably lacking in conflict. The power elite rules, and the masses follow like sheep, with little hope of achieving a "true consciousness." The intellectuals form the strategic strata, not the working class. Mills, after working closely with labor in the late

1940's, abandoned any hope for the working class as an agent of revolutionary change. A few months before he died, Mills reiterated his feelings about the potential of the proletariat.

Marx believed that the working classes in Western Europe would develop into a class-conscious revolutionary force that would overthrow the Capitalists. For Marx, the proletariat was the history making agency. Now any fool can see that it's not true....

Look, in order to develop a New Left, we have to kick this labor metaphysic. No working class in the United States or Western Europe is going to revolt in the foreseeable future.[27]

For Mills, the working class had become a conservative force; neither revolution nor reform would come from it. Giving up on the proletariat, Mills substituted the intellectual and later the young. In his famous "Letter to the New Left" (1960), Mills wondered rhetorically who was "thinking and acting in radical ways. All over the world—in the bloc, outside the bloc and in between—the answer's the same: it is the young intelligensia."[28]

Mills would, of course, die before the internal squabblings and fights together with official repression led to the virtual demise of the New Left in the 1970's.

Most important of all for our purposes is the fact that Mills believed that Marx was an economic determinist in spite of the controversy that has revolved around this interpretation of Marx. Mills is quite explicit about this in *The Marxists*. He summarizes his views in the following passage:

Marx stated clearly the doctrine of economic determinism. It is reflected in his choice of vocabulary; it is assumed by, and fits into, his work as a whole—in particular his theory of power, his conception of state, his rather simple notion of class and the use of these notions (including the proletariat as the agency of history-making). We may of course assume with Engels that he allows a degree of free-play among the several factors that interact, and also that he provides a flexible time schedule in which economic causes do their work. But in the end—and usually the end is not very far off—economic causes are "the basic," the ultimate, the general, the innovative causes of historical change.[29]

Mills was too much of a disciple of Dewey and Weber to accept any form of economic determinism.[30]

Mills's own words attest to the lack of a specific Marxist influence; nevertheless, Marx certainly was an important general influence upon him. Evidence of this can be seen in Mills's radical political commitment, and engagement in a Marxist intellectual ambiance, experiences that neither Weber nor Mannheim had. Irving Louis Horowitz has summed this up:

In truth, Mills was first and foremost a radical. Thus his judgment of Marxism was profoundly influenced by the continued deradicalization of Marx's thought in each of the various socialist pivots of the twentieth century—from the Social Democracy of Bernstein to the Bolshevism of Stalin. It was incumbent upon him to "settle affairs" with Marxism, if only to make clear to himself and to others the exact relationship between the political radicalism of a mid-twentieth century American sociologist and that portion of the "classic tradition" in social science carried on by the Marxists.[31]

This very radicalism led Mills to write for such socialist and leftist periodicals as *Politics, The New Leader, Partisan Review, Labor and Nation,* and *The New Republic* in the 1940's. And when Mills lost his optimism for organized labor, this same radicalism, infused with the pragmatism he never forgot, led him to substitute the intellectual for the proletariat as a possible agent of change.

Marxism, for Mills, is simply a part of the social science tradition, and not, as for some Marxists, the other way around. Mills himself voices this position in *The Marxists,* characterizing himself as a "plain Marxist." Plain Marxists are thinkers who

have emphasized the volition of men in the making of history—their freedom—in contrast to any Determinist Laws of History and, accordingly, the lack of individual responsibility.

In brief, they have confronted the unresolved tension in Marx's work—and in history itself: the tension of humanism and determinism, of human freedom and historical necessity.[32]

In order to analyze class, power, and historical change, the big problems of man in society, one must confront Marx. Like Weber and Mannheim before him, Mills does so, and the influence of Marx is therefore apparent throughout his thought, sometimes to be rejected, other times to be accepted, but always to be contended with.

4

"CHARACTER AND SOCIAL STRUCTURE"

Character and Social Structure (1953) is seminal to an overall understanding of the works of C. Wright Mills. Mills, by focusing upon roles
played in various institutional orders, and how these various institutional
orders combine in a given society to form historical types of social structures, is able to formulate the general model of a social system he had been
calling for since his graduate student days.[1] In short, he synthesizes the
social behaviorism or personality formation of the pragmatists with the
emphasis upon social structure of Max Weber and the German sociologists.

The basic concept in Mills's working model approach is that of role.
Roles by definition are interpersonal; that is, they are oriented to the
expectations of others. These others are also playing roles, and our mutual
expectations set up patterns of social conduct. The individual's psychological functions are thereby shaped by specific configurations of roles
which he has incorporated from his society. The most important aspect of
personality is, of course, the individual's conception of self, or "his idea of
what kind of person he is."[2] The image of self we hold is formulated
through an interpersonal context by taking into account what people think
of us. The approval or disapproval of others acts as a guide in the learning
of both assigned and assumed roles. The internalization of these attitudes
of others enables the individual to gain new roles, and ultimately an image
of self. Roles and one's self-image are entrenched within a social context.
The concept of role through its relationship to institutions provides a link
between the psychology of the individual and the controls of a society. The
model shows the type of person selected and formed by the enactment and
internalization of these roles chosen. Roles make up the social person;

institutions, defined as "... an organization of roles, ... one or more of which is understood to serve the maintenance of the total set of roles,"[3] form the society.

Institutional orders, in the model, are delineated according to function: an institutional order consists of all those institutions which have similar consequences and ends or which serve a similar function. Five major institutional orders make up the skeletal structure of the total society:

1. The *political* order ... consists of those institutions within which men acquire, wield, or influence the distribution of power and authority within social structures.
2. The *economic* order ... is made up of those establishments by which men organize labor, resources, and technical implements in order to produce and distribute goods and services.
3. The *military* order ... is composed of institutions in which men organize legitimate violence and supervise its use.
4. The *kinship* order ... is made up of institutions which regulate and facilitate legitimate sexual intercourse, procreation, and the early bearing of children.
5. The *religious* order is composed of those institutions in which men organize and supervise the collective worship of God or deities, usually at regular occasions and at fixed places.[4]

As stated, symbols, technology, status, and education are the four main spheres of the model. These spheres are defined as follows:

Symbols include signs, emblems, ceremonies, language, music which sustain the order. *Technology* includes tools, apparatus, machines, instruments, and physical devices. *Status* consists of agencies for the means of distributing prestige, deference, or honor. And the *educational* sphere includes activities concerned with the transmission of skills and values to persons who have not yet acquired them.[5]

They are designated spheres because they are rarely autonomous as to the ends they serve, and any of them may be used within any one of the five orders.

A social structure, therefore, consists of institutional orders and spheres; its unity depends upon the relative importance of each institutional order and sphere, and their relation to each other. (See Figure 4.1 for a diagram of Mills's working model.)

Now that Mills's working model has been briefly sketched, we can begin to look at it in depth, focusing first upon his notions of personality formation and then upon his conception of the total model.

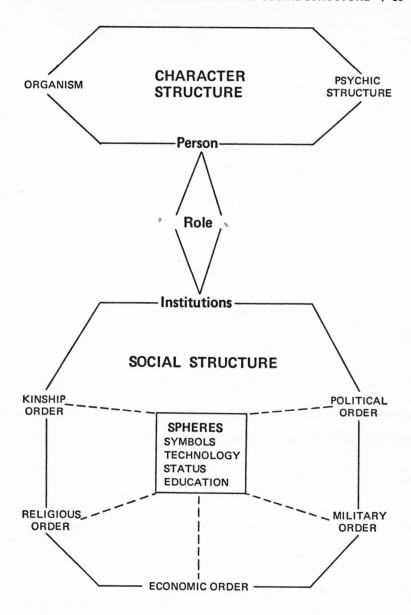

Figure 4-1.
THE COMPONENTS OF C. WRIGHT MILLS'S SOCIAL SYSTEM
Source: C. Wright Mills, "Character and Social Structure" (New York: Harcourt, Brace, and World, 1953), p. 32.

PERSONALITY OR CHARACTER STRUCTURE

Implicit in Mills's model is a model of man. Personality is understood as being anchored in institutional orders which combine to form historical types of social structure. Man is a social creature; biological explanations are inadequate for a full understanding of human beings. Motives rather than stimulus and response are crucial for a comprehensive sociological analysis. "Will," "volition," and "impulse" are the terms of inquiry to be used, and always in a social context. The fundamental question asked is: How, from the standpoint of society, can a person be produced who desires what is socially desirable? Mills's answer is that a cycle is present—a cycle involving undefined impulses and socially available goals. By repetition and suggestion, punishment and reward, impulses are finally integrated with goals. Persons incorporate goals and link them with impulses which sustain the continued operations of the conduct patterns that form various institutions. Human emotions are socially defined. This is the key to Mills's conception of character structure and requires further elaboration.

Emotions

Impulses are shaped and defined by the social situation. The two are linked in that the social situation furnishes an opportunity for the satisfaction of the impulse. The individual internalizes socially defined values and objectives which give direction to impulses, indeed, even set the intensity of these impulses. Impulse becomes purposeful, and conduct is deemed rational.

The meaning of the situation always sets the tone for an individual's emotions. These meanings vary according to the past experiences of the person and are explained in terms of the person's position within given social structures.

Language is the most important mechanism through which the individual becomes aware of his social situation; it is the major avenue for an individual to gain a knowledge of self. Language is a system of signs which are responded to by other persons and also indicate the future actions of the speaker. A given symbol or word can only define the situation for another if it evokes a similar response in that individual. (This, of course, is George Herbert Mead's concept of a significant symbol.)

A person thus consists of an internalization of social roles, with language as *the* mechanism through which this occurs. The individual internalizes the vocal gestures of others and thereby takes on the important features of an interpersonal situation. He draws into his own person those gestures which indicate to him what others expect and require of him. These expectations provide the basis for the development of a self-image.

Images of Self

One's self-image develops and changes through social experiences. The individual is rewarded for certain types of behavior, punished for others. "The self-image which we have at any given time is a reflection of the appraisals of others as modified by our previously developed self."[6] The image a person holds of himself and that held by significant others become integrated and form an individual's self-image. Three basic principles determine the individual's selection of significant others: (1) cumulative confirmations; (2) selection by position and career; (3) the confirming use of the intimate other.

The three principles are integrated in that the social position of the person sets limits for the selection of significant others.

Although these three principles are not the only ones, it is through them that institutions form the personalities of individuals. Put simply, in order to know another's self-image, we must find out those who are significant in his life. The convenient way to gain this knowledge is to look at the circle of significant others with whom the individual comes in contact as he lives out his life in institutional contexts.

When the attitudes of significant others are internalized, they form the "generalized other." As shown previously, Mills modifies somewhat Mead's concept of the generalized other by relating it to institutional orders. As Mills uses the term *generalized other*, it represents the total number of significant others in different institutions. It also follows then that individuals who occupy similar institutional positions would most likely have similar generalized others.

Social types can thus be deduced from roles played in institutions. However, because the concept of role carries with it variations of individual actions, more is needed to understand an individual's character structure. That is, an individual may try to balance out the traits he is called upon to manifest, and he may exhibit different public and private ones. The examples most often given of this are the browbeaten office worker who is a tyrant at home, or the authoritative boss who cowers when his wife speaks. In order to better understand the different types of persons, the model focuses upon motivations.

Motivations

Motives, like emotions, are socially defined. The study of motives revolves around an understanding of the specific directions that human conduct takes. Motives are subjective formulations of action; or, in Max Weber's words, "a motive is a complex of subjective meaning which seems to the actor himself or to the observer an adequate ground for the conduct itself."[7] The problem here is how an investigator can get at these subjective motives. Merely to ask the individual what his motives are might result only in rationalizations. Mills attempts to solve this problem by constructing what he refers to as typical vocabularies of motive which are linked to situated actions. The sociologist simply looks at the typical justification of motives in terms of particular societal frameworks. Examples of this are given in an early paper by Mills:

Individualistic, sexual, hedonistic, and pecuniary vocabularies of motives are apparently now dominant in many sections of twentieth-century urban America. Under such an ethos, verbalization of alternative conduct in these terms is least likely to be challenged among dominant groups. In this milieu, individuals are skeptical of Rockefeller's avowed religious motives for his business conduct because such motives are not *now* terms of the vocabulary conventionally and prominently accompanying situations of business enterprise. A medieval monk writes that he gave food to a poor but pretty woman because it was "for the glory of God and the eternal salvation of his soul." Why do we tend to question him and impute sexual motives? Because sex is an influential and widespread motive in our society and time. Religious vocabularies of explanation and of motives have been debunked on a rather wide scale, certain thinkers are skeptical of those who ubiquitously proclaim them. Religious motives have lapsed from selected portions of modern populations and other motives have become "ultimate" and operative. But from the monasteries of medieval Europe we have no evidence that religious vocabularies were not operative in many situations.[8]

Motives, therefore carry with them specific terminologies which are societally defined for different situations. In order to better understand how motives, as well as emotions and other psychological traits, are defined by one's society we now turn to the social structure part of Mills's model.

SOCIAL STRUCTURE—INSTITUTIONS AND PERSONS

Institutions form persons. An individual's personality is shaped by the various roles he enacts in an institutional framework. Character traits, for instance, are defined by particular institutional orders. What may be considered selfishness in one context might be seen as initiative in another. In Mills's model there are no general psychological traits existing as universals in the character structure; psychological traits are shaped by specific contexts.

The key to the institutional formation of persons lies in the circle of significant others formed by institutions. The individual, in order to succeed in an institution, internalizes the expectations of the institutional leaders; this in turn acts as a means of social control. In time this produces a change in the generalized other of the institutional member. The individual begins to pattern himself after the institutional head, who in the process becomes a significant other. The role and the constraints carried by it become generalized and in this manner become linked psychologically with particular institutions. The ways in which specific traits are joined to institutional contexts can be seen through what Mills calls the theory of premiums and traits of character. This theory has four basic tenets:

1. A general trait that is generally premiumed has a high chance to be presented by the person and to be firmly organized into his character.
2. A specific trait that is generally premiumed will tend to spread, to become a general trait.
3. A general trait that is specifically premiumed will tend to become a specific trait, or, if kept general, to be modified or camouflaged in all contexts except the one in which it is specifically premiumed.
4. A specific trait that is specifically premiumed will tend to be stabilized; a person predominantly composed of such traits will be a compartmentalized specialist.[9]

Institutions place premiums and, of course, taboos on certain traits. For example, educational institutions premium competitiveness. Grades, which are a means of reward in the educational institution, are received by those who compete. The student internalizes the institutionally defined premiums and taboos, sometimes without being aware of their impact upon his personality. The outcome, whether he is aware of it or not, is a competitive individual.

The individual learns these premiums and taboos through the use of language. Language is linked to institutional contexts through the communication process, or, as Mills refers to it, the symbol sphere.

The Symbol Sphere

The symbol sphere, by socially defining the situations an individual confronts, also gives clues to his fears, anxieties, and other psychic elements.

Roles are rejected or accepted by means of symbols. Symbols provide the person with a frame of reference to understand his social experience, a frame of reference which is thereby related to the operation of specific institutions.

There are different types of symbols. The most important are master symbols, which justify the institutional arrangement of an institutional order and are used by those in authority to justify their rule.

Symbols, since they involve specific modes of conduct and the integration of these modes, give rise to special vocabularies. This is discussed in six contexts:

1. The vocabulary is a major element in the style of life which sets off different status groups. . . .
2. In the *economic order,* the jobs that people do together give rise to specialized trade jargons. . . .
3. Families may develop special terms understood only by its members. . . .
4. The symbols of the *political order* may be visual or auditory, like the flag or the national anthem, or they may be sentimentalized places like the Capitol or written documents as in the constitutional states of modern democracies. . . .
5. The symbol spheres of the *military order* and of the political order are blended in the modern national state. . . .
6. In the *religious order* the symbol sphere is very important, since the contents with which religion deals and the sanctions it employs are "psychic." [10]

The Status Sphere

There is very little difference between what Mills calls the status sphere and Max Weber's famous conception of stratification. All Mills does is round out Weber's unfinished dimension of occupation and add it to the class, status, and party trichotomy. The four dimensions of stratification are related to institutional orders and to the social structure in that they represent ways of focusing upon specific features of roles in various institutional orders. They are both interrelated and interdependent.

An occupation is any set of activities that provide a livelihood. Occupations are economic roles and, although found in other institutional orders, they are usually located in the economic institutional order. Occupations are skills that are marketable from the individual's standpoint and functional from the standpoint of society. Mills's primary interest here is with occupational shifts in American society, as witnessed in *White Collar,* where he traces the decline of the old middle class (the independent entrepreneur) and the rise of the new middle class (the salaried employee).

The class structure is anchored to the amount of wealth, to property institutions, and to the occupational roles found within economic institutions. In Mills's scheme, laws of property are part and parcel of the political order of the society. Those classes which can be labelled property classes could not exist only in terms of economic institutions; they must be dealt with as facts of a political economy.

The status sphere involves prestige claimed by certain individuals as well as others who honor the claim. Status can be claimed in any order, and because individuals enact roles in more than one order, their status usually rests upon a combination of roles. Of the four dimensions of stratification, status is the most relevant to the psychology of the individual. It is directly connected to the self-esteem of the person.

Power, the last of the four dimensions, while intertwined with the other three, more often than not defines them. Power is almost always political power. Class, status, and occupation are spokes; power, the wheel.

THE UNITY OF SOCIAL STRUCTURES

Mills, always the sociologist, demonstrates his concern with total social structures by advancing four ideal type models of integration.

The institutions composing a social structure may be unified by *correspondence* (the several institutional orders develop in accordance with a common principle), by *coincidence* (various institutional developments lead to a similar resultant end) by *coordination* (one institutional order becomes dominant over the others and manages them) and by *convergence* (in their development, one or more institutional orders blend).[11]

Correspondence is best exemplified by the classic liberal society which prevailed in the United States during the first half of the nineteenth century. An example of *coincidence* is best seen in Max Weber's famous treatise on Protestantism and capitalism.

The example given by Mills for *coordination* is America in the 1950s. (This is what *The Power Elite* is all about). Frontier America in the nineteenth-century illustrates *convergence*.

CRITICS OF THE MODEL

Up to now I have not offered any criticism of Mills's general model. My reason, quite simply, is that Mills's integration of the individual's personality with his social structure is fundamentally a viable one. Where Mills went wrong was not with the model but with certain applications of it. The working model itself is an excellent heuristic device which can be used to interpret why man acts as he does in given situations. This interpretation is, of course, not the only one. Elliot Mishler, for instance, sees Mills's working model as extremely sketchy, offering an inadequate treatment of personality, only one major descriptive construct (the self), only one mechanism (language), and only one "crude" behavioral law (a form of reward learning).[12] Basically, Mishler's criticisms are too harsh. First of all, while Mills does offer only one descriptive construct, it is made up of three other constructs: organism, psychic structure, and person. An integrated character structure is postulated, something rare among most sociological views of man. As for the use of only one mechanism, language, this is a misinterpretation of Mills. Mills's position was that the use of language is the most important mechanism and the major source of the individual's knowledge of self, not the only one. The importance of language in coordinating social behavior is so generally accepted that we need not concern ourselves with it here.

This brings us to Mishler's last point, that Mills uses only one behavioral law (reward learning). In *Character and Social Structure,* Mills not only does not postulate behavioral laws, he specifically relativizes what passes for such in the psychological literature. Take, for example, Mills's theory of premiums and traits of character. There are no general principles of character structure in terms of how one trait will lead to the selection of other traits. There are no general character traits which exist as universals; they must be seen as tied to given ranges of social situations. Even anxiety, which is central to the theory of interpersonal behavior of Harry Stack Sullivan, from whom Mills borrowed the concept of "significant other," is seen as being socially relative. In Sullivan's theory the individual develops a self-system whose basic function is to avoid anxiety. Mills takes what is a behavioral law for Sullivan and shows that anxiety is better understood in relation to an institutional framework. Fear and anxiety cannot be separated from the object feared. What to fear, that which produces the anxiety, is historically given and socially learned. Anxiety might range from that produced by the fear of illegitimate children in the kinship order to the fear of bankruptcy in the economic order. Social conditions lead to conditions of anxiety and, on the other side of the coin, also channel those compensations which relieve anxieties. In a word, Mills's "laws" cannot be understood in terms of reward and learning.

A more valid criticism is offered by Ernest Becker, who writes that "an adequate theory of personality must show man pulling and straining against himself; it must reveal a man who is somehow less than fully socialized—which amounts to the same thing."[13] Does Mills offer, then, what amounts to "an oversocialized conception of man?"[14] Perhaps so.

But this need not detract from the usefulness of the model, for Mills offers a paradigm for the formation of social types, with the implication that the social psychologist focus upon polar or extreme types. While Mills may not specifically have left us a picture of an individual straining against himself, as Becker calls for, his paradigm of social types shifts the level of analysis to the social-psychological rather than the purely psychological. And herein lies Mills's contribution. Like Weber before him, Mills is interested in the historical formation of social types. His working model enables him to focus upon these social types. If he does not present a fully integrated theory of personality, he certainly defines the direction it must take— it must consider the biological organism, the psychic structure, and the person.

In sum, *Character and Social Structure* represents Mills's attempt to combine the pragmatist's conception of personality with the sociologist's notion of social structure. Mills offers a full-blown model of man and society, an historical social-psychological framework which tells us why man acts the way he does in any given epoch. After *Character and Social Structure* his works take on a different slant. *The Power Elite*, for instance, written three years after *Character and Social Structure*, is an application of the theory of power based upon the model, as is *The Causes of World War III*. *The Sociological Imagination* and *The Marxists* represent critiques of other models using the general model of a social system as a basis for the critique.

Mills's works, then, after *Character and Social Structure*, move in a definite direction. After the model was completed, the next step was to use it.

5

THE SOCIOLOGY OF KNOWLEDGE

The sociology of knowledge represents one of Mills's earliest intellectual interests. With the exception of a 1957 article entitled "The Cultural Apparatus" and certain statements which can be culled from *The Sociological Imagination* (1959), all of his works in this area were written while he was a graduate student at the University of Wisconsin, all before he reached the age of twenty-five. The articles "Language, Logic, and Culture" (1939), "Methodological Consequences of the Sociology of Knowledge" (1940), "The Language and Ideas of Ancient China: Marcel Granet's Contribution to the Sociology of Knowledge" (1940), "Situated Actions and Vocabularies of Motive" (1940), "The Professional Ideology of Social Pathologists" (1943),[1] and Mills's doctoral dissertation, "A Sociological Account of Pragmatism" (1942), posthumously published as *Sociology and Pragmatism* (1964), contain Mills's views on the sociology of knowledge.

Mills's foray in the field of the sociology of knowledge is directly related to his attempted synthesis of pragmatism and German sociology. Because the bulk of his work in this area was written at the beginning of his career, the articles are more heavily imbued with pragmatism than are his later works. Mills did temper his pragmatism with a call for a notion of social structure, though, and therein we can see the beginnings of his attempted synthesis. Written before he completed his model, these early articles have a different stamp from the much later "Cultural Apparatus" and *The Sociological Imagination*.

The position taken here augments that of Irving Louis Horowitz, who points out in his introduction to *Sociology and Pragmatism* that Mills's

sociology of knowledge is infused with the influence of the American pragmatists, particularly Peirce, Mead, and Dewey.[2] This constitutes a unique
approach by Mills to the sociology of knowledge. Horowitz calls attention
to this when he writes about Mills's coining the word *sociotics:*

By designating his work as "sociotics," Mills sought to encompass all sociological phenomena involved in the function of language; the ways in which
language channelizes and elicits thought. But as Mills readily acknowledges,
sociotics derives from the work of Charles W. Morris in the *Foundations
of the Theory of Signs.* It is nothing more than the relation of signs to their
users—what Morris calls pragmatics—seen from a sociological perspective.
From this vantage point, rather than from Marx or Mannheim, Mills came
to a study of the sociology of knowledge. This is why we find Mills empha-
sizing the social basis for the *discovery of truth,* rather than the economic
basis for the *uncovering of error.*[3]

Mills's position is that from the standpoint of the sociology of knowledge, the question of truth or falsity is still an important one, although it
is taken for granted that truth or falsity cannot be deduced from an individual's social position. Mannheim's formulation of the sociology of
knowledge, which has dominated the discipline in the English-speaking
world,[4] could explain how ideas emerged, but not whether they are true
or false. Mannheim's confrontation with untruth can be summarized as
follows:

All the ideas which do not fit into the current order are "situationally
transcendent" or unreal. Ideas which correspond to the concretely existing
and *de facto* order are designated as "adequate" and situationally congruous. . . . Contrasted with situationally congruous and adequate ideas are
the two main categories of ideas which transcend the situation—ideologies
and utopia. . . . This conception of ideology (and utopia) maintains that
beyond the commonly recognized sources of error we must also reckon
with the effects of a distorted mental structure.
    . . . In the same historical epoch and in the same society there may be
several distorted types of inner mental structures, some because they have
not yet grown up to the present and others because they are already beyond
the present. In either case the reality to be comprehended is distorted and
concealed.[5]

Mannheim's position was that knowledge could only be knowledge from
a certain perspective, and he constantly sought *the* social standpoint which
offered the optimal choice for finding truth. Mannheim's attempt at solving
this problem was the borrowing of Alfred Weber's notion of the "socially
unattached intelligentsia"—those individuals who, because they had no
particular ax to grind, could rise above social determinants of thought. What

Mannheim failed, or refused, to see was that the intelligentsia are a class like any other, and far from being unattached, are tied to a specific location, world view, and set of interests just like anyone else.[6] On balance, then, Mannheim's solution seems only slightly better than Marx's proletariat—the class that would overcome "false-consciousness."

In brief, Mannheim's dilemma is a logical outgrowth of his essential principle of historicism—that of relativism. Though he believed relativism to be all there was to reality, Mannheim, a product of an idealistic social science tradition, could never fully rid himself of a yearning for an absolute.[7] This unhappiness with relativism merely led to a substitution of the term "relationism," by which Mannheim meant: "If we formulate a truth, we do so in abstract and absolute terms, but always include in the formula the concrete conditions to which it is related, i.e., under which it really holds true."[8] Hoping to shake the specter of relativism, Mannheim was reduced to a play on words. Finally all he could do was abandon this pursuit and adopt an activist, atheoretical attitude. Mannheim's ultimate criterion of truth became that of the American pragmatists—action. In his *Essays on the Sociology of Knowledge,* Mannheim wrote: "Only a philosophy which is able to give a concrete answer to the question 'what shall we do?' can put forth the claim to have overcome relativism."[9] Werner Stark has summed up quite well Mannheim's position on truth-action:

... With Mannheim the ... question is whether they [an individual's ideas] enable him to act harmoniously in his society. If ideologies and utopias are both unrealistic, the former because they are behind, the latter because they are ahead of the times, then it follows that realistic thought is that which is fully adjusted to the times, and this means as Mannheim himself explains, that it is thought which works in "hitchlessly" ... with the established social pattern, the ongoing social process.[10]

Adherence to the actual and adjustment to the given constellation of things are the two operating concepts in Mannheim's epistemology.

C. WRIGHT MILLS AND THE SOCIOLOGY OF KNOWLEDGE

Mills's contribution to the sociology of knowledge begins at the point where Mannheim embraced pragmatism. Mills expanded Mannheim's assertion that truth is what works and showed that even "what works" is socially determined. By combining Mannheim's sociology of knowledge with the American pragmatists' emphasis on verification models, Mills offers an analysis of what passes for truth in any given situation. The word *true,* from Mills's perspective, is "an adjective applied to propositions that satisfy the forms of an accepted model of verification."[11] In this manner, Mills's sociology of knowledge can even refer to degrees of truth, because it includes conditions under which statements can be judged true or false. The sociologist's job is to point out the conditions affecting the use of one verification model over another. Although the social position of the thinker does not affect the truthfulness of the propositions being tested by the verification model, social position is still an important consideration in that it may well affect whether or not one type of model is used as opposed to another. The verification scheme is itself socially relativized, its selection open to sociological verification. Verification models are ideological, and Mills's sociology of knowledge analyzes this ideology. Rather than deal with error, as did Mannheim and Marx, Mills deals with the very structure of the constitutional framework essential to any analysis of the social basis for discovering truth. Mills, unlike Mannheim, embraces relativism completely, analyzing how relative truth becomes institutionalized. This is done by focusing upon two areas: the sociology of language and the sociology of truth and validity.

The Sociology of Language

The social determination of ideas is dependent upon social-psychological questions, in particular the impact of social structure on the mind of an individual. According to Mills, most sociologists following the leads of Marx and Mannheim had overlooked psychological considerations for the sociology of language. Marx and his followers used psychological terms which were question-begging and noninclusive, and Mannheim covered up his psychological inadequacies with a vague and unanalyzed "collective unconsciousness."[12]

In order to formulate a theory that incorporates the social-psychological aspects of a sociology of knowledge, the importance of the social process of thought must be stressed—in particular the work of the American pragmatists, who held that thinking follows the pattern of language. An internalized organization of collective attitudes develops through conversation, which, in turn, enables ideas to be logically tested. Reason and logic are derived from a social standpoint. An individual is considered logical only if he is in general agreement with members of his universe of discourse in relation to the validity of some general notion of what constitutes logic.

The influence of Charles Sanders Peirce is readily apparent in the thought of Mills. Compare Mills's statements on logic with this passage from Peirce's "What Pragmatism Is":

Two things here are important to insure oneself of and to remember. The first is that a person is not absolutely an individual. His thoughts are what he is "saying to himself," that is, is saying to that other self that is just coming into life in the flow of time. When one reasons, it is that self that one is trying to persuade; and all thought whatsoever is a sign, and is mostly of the nature of language. The second thing to remember is that man's circle of society (however widely or narrowly this phrase may be understood) is a sort of loosely compacted person, in some respects of higher rank than the person of an individual organism. It is these two things alone that render it possible for you—but only in the abstract, and in a Pickwickian sense—to distinguish between absolute truth and what you do not doubt.[13]

Language is social because words assume meaning only when they are interpreted by social behavior. Social patterns establish meaning. Language sets the basis for reason, logic, and by extension all scientific endeavor. Put simply, one is logical when one is in agreement with one's universe of discourse. This relativistic posture enabled Mills to develop a view of the function of language as a mediator of social behavior and as a system of social control.

Words carry meanings by virtue of dominant interpretations placed upon them by social behavior. Interpretations or meanings spring from the habitual modes of behavior which pivot upon symbols. Such social patterns of behavior constitute the meanings of symbols.[14]

Thought comes under the control of language, and along with a language come values and norms. Value judgments and collective patterns exist behind words; meaning is socially bestowed. The individual acquires a "vocabulary of motive." This concept of vocabulary of motive, introduced by Mills in "Language, Logic, and Culture" and expanded in "Situated Actions and Vocabularies of Motive," points out how motives can be considered as typical vocabularies which have established and ascertainable functions in delimited social situations.[15] This approach parallels that of Mead, who had also attacked Wundt's notion of language as the expression of prior elements within the mind of the individual. Mead in this manner sought to explain conduct both from within and without. Motives are linked to situations. For Mills, this is accomplished through "the construction of typical vocabularies of motives that are extant in types of situations and actions. Imputation of motives may be controlled by reference to the typical constellation of motives which are observed to be societally linked with classes of situated actions."[16] Examples of this are those vocabularies which tend to be characteristic of particular epochs. Sexual, individualistic, and hedonistic would characterize American society at mid-century, whereas religious vocabularies of motives would be found in the Middle Ages.

"Situated Actions and Vocabularies of Motive" is a pivotal article in Mills's sociology of knowledge. Here Mills, via a modification of Dewey's view of impulses as constituents of habit, goes beyond pragmatism to a more structural world view than that of Mead and Dewey. Using the concept of role, which not only tells the individual how to act but also satisfies his need for the reflected appraisals of others, Mills locates vocabularies of motive in historical situations. Motives have no value apart from the social situation.

In "Situated Actions and Vocabularies of Motive" as well as in "Language, Logic, and Culture," Mills lays out a broad theoretical framework for a sociology of language which incorporates a social-psychological viewpoint into the sociology of knowledge. Though he hints at a methodology which would enable the sociologist to work within the sociology of knowledge, Mills does not spell one out until much later. The closest he comes to doing so in these early works is through his introduction of the term *sociotics* in "The Language and Ideas of Ancient China." The concept demarcates for analysis: "(a) all the sociological phenomena that are involved in the functioning of language, and (b) the ways by which lingual phenomena channel, limit, and elicit thought."[17] *Sociotics* is a portion of a theory of language as well as a division in the sociology of knowledge.

In "The Language and Ideas of Ancient China," Mills analyzes Marcel Granet's *La Civilization Chinoise* and *La Pensée Chinoise* in light of Granet's notions of the functional aspects of language. Language is a social creation and exercises a powerful influence on thinking. Society defines reality for the individual, and language is the mechanism through which the individual learns of this reality. Granet's writings are used to substantiate this position because, employing a Durkheimian frame of reference, Granet had attempted to explain thought and ideas in terms of a social system.

The relationship between language and scientific thought is of particular interest to Mills. Granet's findings show that due to the Chinese notion of a particular order which presides over all of life there is nothing in the Chinese mentality equivalent to the Western concept of rationalism. This order realizes itself in a belief in the essential harmony of man and nature, something foreign to Western thought. Society and the universe manifest the same order. Causality, which is basic to scientific endeavor, is missing in the Chinese system. It is replaced by the principle of Tao, which invokes a totality and unity of order. Nor is time conceived of as continuous duration and separate from space.

The collective representations of time and space constitute a framework for the total art of ruling. They supported an art of merging, by symbol and ritual, the world and the society of humans at its center. There is nothing about them which even faintly suggests the employment of categories in the organization of abstract thought which has been among Western thinkers a predominant ideal.[18]

The idea of a finished universe, a unification of man and nature, dominates Chinese thought. Society defines language, and language defines man's behavior and thinking. This is Granet's contribution to the sociology of knowledge; a view that fits in nicely with Mills's on the subject. .

The Sociology of Truth and Validity

Mills's second endeavor in these early articles revolves around his desire to formulate a social basis for the discovery of truth. This involves a different point of departure from the traditional sociology of knowledge. Although Mills agrees that knowing the social position of the thinker does not enable one to deduce the truth or validity of his statements, he is nevertheless convinced that the question of truth is relevant in terms of accepted models or systems of verification. He therefore attempts to incorporate verification models proposed by Peirce and Dewey with a sociology which takes into account the social position of the thinker.

Before we can judge whether or not Mills succeeded in accomplishing what he set out to do, the verification models of the pragmatists must be examined.

Charles Sanders Peirce

According to Peirce, knowledge must fit the model of scientific statements. He writes:

To satisfy our doubts, therefore, it is necessary that a method should be found by which our beliefs may be caused by nothing human, but by some external permanency—by something upon which our thinking has no effect. . . . This is the method of science. Its fundamental hypothesis, restated in more familiar language, is this: There are real things, whose character are entirely independent of our opinions about them; these realities affect our senses according to regular laws, and though our sensations are as different as are our relations to the objects, yet, by taking advantage of the laws of perception, we can ascertain by reasoning how things really and truly are; and any man, if he have sufficient experience and he reason enough about it, will be led to the one true conclusion.[19]

Truth is discovered by using the scientific method. Every contribution to knowledge must be able to withstand the inquiries of other scientists. Implicit in Peirce's conception of truth is the belief that if investigation into any problem is carried far enough, one solution will establish itself as logically superior to all the others. That is all that truth is, according to Peirce.[20] In his words, "the opinion which is fated to be ultimately agreed to by all who investigate, is what we mean by truth, and the object represented in this opinion is the real one. This is the way I would explain reality."[21] Peirce's notion of truth—or to use Mills's terms, Peirce's verification model—rests upon a consensus of opinion ultimately arrived at by investigating scientists.

John Dewey

The influence of Dewey's verification model upon Mills's early works is even more pronounced than that of Peirce's. Knowledge for Dewey is simply another name for the product of competent inquiries. Apart from this, its meaning is empty. Dewey never uses the term *truth*. An interpretor of Dewey comments on this point:

"Truth" is a word so overladen with traditional metaphysics that to use it would incur the risk of beclouding the whole issue. So instead of using it, Dewey came to the point of saying that an idea that is found valid in inquiry is one we are "warranted" in accepting, one we "assert" with confidence— "truth" thereby becoming "warranted assertibility."[22]

What is important to Dewey, therefore, is the scientific context of inquiry; that which can be confirmed by principles of scientific inquiry.

Dewey's "verification theory of truth" holds that something is true if it agrees with experience as shown through scientific methods of inquiry. This is the point at which Dewey and Peirce differ somewhat. For Peirce, this does not necessarily have to be. His idea of truth is based on a mathematical model. Dewey's, on the other hand, is tied up more completely with the method. In *The Quest for Certainty* Dewey writes:

The scientist finds no help in determining the probable truth of some proposed theory by comparing it with an absolute standard of truth and immutable being. He has to rely upon definite operations undertaken under definite conditions—upon method.[23]

By combining validity with method, Dewey opens up the problem of multiple "truths." "One might even go as far as to say that there are as many kinds of valid knowledge as there are conclusions wherein distinctive operations have been employed to solve the problems set by antecedently experienced situations."[24]

Dewey's position represents a break with the notion that the mind knows because it is a spectator to reality. For Dewey, thought is spatio-temporal. Eternal truths, universals, *a priori* systems are suspect. Experience is considered to be the experience of the environment—an environment that is physical, biological, and cultural. Ideas do not belong to a world of their own, are not Platonic essences, but are functional to the experience of the individual. The individual mind along with the object is a partner in the experience of knowing. Dewey adds the notion of science to the problem of knowing. A. H. Somjee calls Dewey's method "trial-and-error" rationality.

The rationale of trial-and-error procedure is fully embodied in the method of science. Science accepts a theory only after subjecting it to its own tests and also acknowledges only a statistical, not an absolute confirmation. In doing so, it not only subjects a theory to trial but acknowledges that its own testing procedure is itself on trial.

Science consists of a body of hypotheses that are confirmed or confirmable in different degrees. For those hypotheses that are confirmed today, science admits a possibility of their refutation tomorrow. . . . By an endless procedure of formulating and testing hypotheses and also by repeatedly testing the correctness of its own methods of testing, science has evolved the most dependable form of knowledge that human beings have known so far. Behind its method lies its conviction that there is no other more reliable method possible than the method of trial and error. All that we can do with what we regard as an intellectually correct and practically sound hypothesis is to subject it to a process of intelligent trial and careful detection of its errors.[25]

This trial-and-error model of truth is essentially the verification model that Mills writes about in "Methodological Consequences of the Sociology of Knowledge."

MILLS'S SOCIOLOGICAL ASSERTIONS AND THE VERIFICATION MODELS

Mills, trained as a sociologist, circumvented the absolutist dilemma of the pragmatists. The sociologist of knowledge could refer to degrees of truth because he includes conditions under which things can be judged true or false. It is his job to point out the conditions under which things can be judged true or false. It is his job to point out the conditions affecting the use of one verification model over another. The social position of the thinker becomes important because, while not affecting the truthfulness of the propositions being tested by the verification model, it does affect whether or not one type model is used as opposed to another.

Truth, from the perspective of the sociology of knowledge, is as stated before only applied to propositions which in turn satisfy accepted models of verification. Mills's sociology of knowledge incorporates Dewey's identification of epistemology with methodology.

This realization carries the belief that the deriving of norms from one type of inquiry (even though it have wide prestige, e.g., "physical science") is not the end of epistemology. In its "epistemological function" the sociology of knowledge is specifically propaedeutic to the construction of sound methodology for the social sciences.[26]

Problems of value are also central to methodological concerns and are to be dealt with through a sociological analysis of the specific disciplines within which the problems arise. Mills does just this when he singles out the field of social pathology and asks how the predominantly academic position of American sociologists affects the research models used to verify their work. By asking this question at the end of "Methodological Consequences," Mills delineates an area where the sociology of knowledge might deal with empirical problems.

The emphasis placed by American sociologists upon continuous process as a central category leads to a failure to study dislocations in social change. The sociologist of knowledge is in a position to investigate why this occurs and in doing so elucidate the social basis for the discovery of truth. In this way Mills deals with the categories of discourse and their relationship to social structure, as well as with the social nature of perception. Following Dewey's emphasis on the identification of epistemology with methodology, Mills writes:

The detailed self-location of social science, if systematically and sensitively performed, not only will lead to detection of errors in methods under way but constructively will result in presentation of sounder paradigms for future research.[27]

"The Professional Ideology of Social Pathologists" is an empirical investigation into the nature of the social perception of the social pathologists and their relation to their social structure. In this article Mills uncovers the social orientation which produced the style of thought common to the textbooks of the 1920's and 1930's in social pathology. The low level of abstraction found in the textbooks is traced to the authors' neglect of total social structures. The social pathologists had similar backgrounds and careers and because of this general homogeneity never developed divergent points of view.

It is clear that Mills is interested in placing the social pathologists in their socio-historical context, a procedure that would become an integral part of his working model approach.

The ideal of practicality, of not being "utopian," operated, in conjunction with other factors, as a polemic against the "philosophy of history" brought into American sociology by men trained in Germany; this polemic implemented the drive to lower levels of abstraction. A view of isolated and immediate problems as the "real" problems may well be characteristic of a society rapidly growing and expanding, as America was in the nineteenth century, and, ideologically, in the early twentieth century.[28]

Social pathology textbook authors had defined problems in terms of the prevailing norms of the society. These norms are never examined by the authors and are therefore tacitly sanctioned. The question of why these norms are violated is answered in an organismic way and more socialization is offered as the solution to the problems raised by any violation of the norms. The social pathologists were not aware of the normative structure within which so-called social problems lay, and this reflected an inherent bias that the sociologist of knowledge could get at. He, using the pragmatist's notion of verification models, holds the particular model of truth up to scrutiny. This is Mills's purpose in this article. The social pathologist could not see the problem as a whole because of the particular situations, roles, and institutions in which he was immersed. Institutions train people for the roles they are to play. In terms of Mills's overall model, institutions produce specific types of personalities which are best suited for the particular institution. Institutions of the time were training judges and social workers to see problems in terms of situations, not structural wholes. The social pathologists were tied to these other professions, trained like them by the case study method. Similarities of background and institutional selection would not allow divergencies to come to the fore. The experiences of the social pathologists, their orientations, were too similar to permit any controversies that might have led to the construction of a holistic approach. The social biographies of the social pathologists are related to the institutions which comprise their particular social structure, in this case American society in the 1920's and 1930's. The individual's character and the social structure within which he acts out his institutional roles shape his social perception. The social pathologists constitute a social type—the method for analyzing their behavior (in this case, textbook writing) is the same that would be used for labor leaders, white-collar workers, members of the power elite, and academics. Roles and mutual expectations set up patterns of social conduct and social perception. The social pathologists are "significant others" to each other. In order to succeed, they internalize institutional expectations. A primary example of this is the audience or public for which the textbooks are written. Sociology, addressing an audience composed primarily of college students and having to justify its existence in competition with other academic disciplines, would of necessity need an emphasis upon presentation and justification rather than on the context of discovery. Writing in this manner is premiumed and eventually becomes accepted. The milieux that the social pathologist finds himself in, the institutions that shape his thoughts and values, predispose him to treat the concept of social pathology in the manner Mills describes.

Mills's analysis is interesting in that it adds something to the sociology of knowledge—it locates and holds up for criticism the models of truth and verification the social pathologists accept. By tracing their backgrounds, Mills is able to point out how a similarity of experience leads to an acceptance of a particular notion of truth. Using the insights of Peirce and Dewey, Mills offers a different approach to the sociology of knowledge. He criticizes the social pathologists for their failure to take the concept of social structure into account, and he traces the reasons for this. Mills combines the pragmatist's notion of the methodological verification of truth with the sociologist's emphasis on the relationship of the individual's perception to his social structure. Like Mannheim, Mills sees the thought of every group arising out of its life conditions. Specific biases in the social situation had influenced the thought of the social pathologists. Mills's contribution is the notion that the verification model used is itself ideological and therefore subject to social determinants.[29]

Mills, unlike Mannheim, embraces relativism totally. Truth is probabilistic; the sociology of knowledge analyzes the degree and the conditions under which statements are to be judged true or false. Relativism, used this way, leads the investigator to an understanding of the conditions under which relative statements can be taken as "true."

Mills, with the help of the pragmatists, takes a step beyond Mannheim and the German school of the sociology of knowledge with his emphasis upon the probabilistic nature of "models of truth" used in scientific investigation. This same theme is taken up in a slightly different form in Mills's doctoral dissertation, "A Sociological Account of Pragmatism," where he is concerned not with the truth of pragmatism *per se,* but with its institutionalization, an institutionalization related to the manner in which the roles of the pragmatists were intertwined within the socio-historical context of the American university in the late nineteenth century.

A Sociological Account of Pragmatism

In "A Sociological Account of Pragmatism" (1942), Mills's doctoral dissertation, published in 1964 as *Sociology and Pragmatism: The Higher Learning in America,* Mills zeroes in on the manner in which pragmatism as a philosophy became institutionalized in the American university.

Mills himself writes that the major problem in his dissertation consists of

explaining the relations between one type of philosophy, Pragmatism and the American social structure, "between" philosophy and society; operating as a crude but most tangible link are the educational institutions of higher learning. The professionalization of philosophy within American institutions of learning is the most obvious social anchorage of the field. . . . From the standpoint of higher education we can study the changing social structure and the shiftings of philosophical doctrines.[30]

Mills accomplishes this by focusing upon the three most famous and influential thinkers in American pragmatism, Peirce, James, and Dewey. The history of pragmatism is, in part, a history of the academic profession in American higher education. This is so because pragmatism, particularly in its later stages, focused intellectually upon what was occurring in the policy and organizational practice of educational institutions.

Charles Sanders Peirce is seen by Mills as outside the major trend in the philosophy of his time, transcendentalism. The "sociological" reason for this was that Peirce was never fully integrated into the academic world, remaining at best a marginal being in academia throughout his life. Peirce's father, one of the foremost mathematicians of his day, was regarded by Mills as contributing to C. S. Peirce's scientific interest in the study of philosophy. The two major factors to consider in Peirce's career are thus his standing as an active scientist and his position as an outsider in philosophy. Throughout his career Peirce was always outside the major institutions of American philosophy, and this had a profound effect upon his thinking. Because he was an active scientist he did not accept the prevailing models of philosophical truth and always held to a position which stressed scientific practice in action and methodology. Mills's methodology in his dissertation is similar to that used in "Professional Ideology"; he seeks the social basis for the acceptance or, in Peirce's case, the nonacceptance of the accepted notions of truth. Peirce, an outsider and a scientist, developed a direct link between abstract thought and concepts of action.

William James, a professor at Harvard whose extensive writings placed him at the center of the academic world, required an interpretive perspective slightly different from that used to understand Peirce. James functioned primarily as a popularizer of pragmatism. The key to his impact on the pragmatic school was his sensitivity to the requirements of a larger and less specialized audience. Peirce's work appeared in scholarly and technical journals; James wrote for the public at large. Mills also claims that James's religious beliefs led him away from the scientific position of Peirce to an emphasis upon personal experience. James's pragmatism moved from the laboratory to the personal level, the real level for pragmatic testing. James's biography is related to his social structure by the variables of "public" and "religious beliefs."

As he had examined the religious background of James, Mills looks at John Dewey's religious beliefs and concludes that Dewey only nominally accepted the religious notions of his time, that religion had not been at all influential in his thought. Dewey's graduate training in philosophy at Johns Hopkins was much more important. He studied under George S. Morris, one of the few teachers of philosophy in the United States who was not a clergyman.

As in his analysis of Peirce and James, Mills addresses himself to the publics Dewey reached, considering four: (1) the social and political; (2) the technical-philosophical; (3) the educational; and (4) the student.[31] Mills's analysis of Dewey's relation to his political public shows just what he was trying to do. Mills asks whether the fact that the political publics Dewey addressed did not have any political aspirations affected Dewey's conception of action, which was on the whole a very cautious one. Adjustment was the key term; violence was considered wasteful. Dewey was mugwumpish in politics, and his conception of action was never linked to any political organization.

Dewey's politics had not taken the form of party politics. In Mills's view, this was to be expected of anyone who was faithful to experimental philosophy. These expectations were further related to the social structure within which Dewey worked.

In short, the assimilation of problems of political power and of moral goods to a statement of thinking, of method, to a model of action and thought imputed to "science," occurred within the social context of a growing industrialization that was spreading across a physical continent and from the position of one in close, daily contact with the rising professional and skilled groups who were central in the implementation of this conquest of nature by machine.

This model was highlighted by the many fingers pointing at the technological results of science and from the success of professions implemented by them. But the model is generalized by Dewey into education and into the discussion of politics. In these contexts and particularly in the latter, "scientific method" becomes "the *method* of intelligence" and this method is equated with "liberal democracy."[32]

In this manner, Mills analyzes the social aspects of what can easily be referred to as Dewey's vocabulary of motives.

In short, in his doctoral dissertation, Mills tries to show how the social biographies of America's pragmatists were related to the social structure of the United States in the late nineteenth century. Peirce, the son of a famous mathematician, working outside of academia, formulated the scientific beginnings of pragmatism. James, pragmatism's popularizer, found his locus for testing in the personal and moral sphere. And Dewey, at the center of the academic world, was in a position to envision a utopian mode of practice, thereby formulating a type of thought intrinsically related to his academic status.

If there is a weakness in Mills's argument it is that his conception of social structure is not fully developed. Mills treats the individual thinkers as unique. Biographies, careers, social circles, publics are all analyzed as dependent variables with little or no connection made. The analysis of Peirce's, James's, and Dewey's relationships to the institutionalization of pragmatism in America is first-rate, as is the tangential analysis of the sociological implications of their thought; but they are, unfortunately, separate analyses. Mills shows the relationship between pragmatism and American higher education but does not spell out the sociological implications of the relationship. He is not able to do so because his model is not fully developed at this time.

But Mills does make a significant contribution to the sociology of knowledge in "A Sociological Account of Pragmatism." He shows how a particular model of truth, pragmatism in this instance, came to be accepted in academic circles. Embellishing the framework laid out in "Methodological Consequences" and "Professional Ideology," Mills traces the special determinants that led to the institutionalization of a verification model, producing "not a study in the *truth* of pragmatism but rather a study in its utility."[33] If Mills had done nothing else but write these two articles and his doctoral dissertation, his investigations into the ideological nature of verification models would have established him as an important contributor to the sociology of knowledge.

MILLS'S LATER WRITINGS IN THE SOCIOLOGY OF KNOWLEDGE

"The Cultural Apparatus" (1957) is important for understanding Mills's later thoughts on the sociology of knowledge because: (1) it is the only article Mills wrote in the area of the sociology of knowledge after his model was formulated; and (2) it represents a stepping stone to ideas developed at greater length in *The Sociological Imagination.*[34]

Written late in Mills's career, "The Cultural Apparatus" has a definite notion of a social structure, a conception based upon the working model of a social system devised in *Character and Social Structure*. The contrast between the early articles and "The Cultural Apparatus" is quite stark, for in the early articles Mills's attempts at defining the term *social structure* are amorphous, almost as unstructured as Dewey's use of *culture*, and he uses the term interchangeably with *sociological setting, social coordinates, societal frames,* and *societal structures.*

In "The Cultural Apparatus" on the other hand, *social structure* is defined as an integration of institutional orders, with the cultural apparatus mediating between social biography and social milieux. By the term *cultural apparatus* Mills means

all the organizations and milieux in which artistic, intellectual and scientific work is made available to circles, publics, and masses. . . . Inside this apparatus, standing between men and events, the images, meaning, slogans, the worlds in which men live are organized, hidden, debunked, celebrated. Taken as a whole, the cultural apparatus is the lens of mankind through which men see; the medium through which they interpret and report what they see. It is the semiorganized source of their very identities and of their aspirations. It is the source of The Human Variety—of styles of life and of ways to die.[35]

Truth is that which is defined by the cultural apparatus. When Mills writes that "the cultural apparatus as a whole is established and used by the dominant institutional orders."[36] he is basing his views on his working model, his integration of individuals and institutions.

The cultural apparatus is controlled by the establishment, by those in authority. In relation to *The Power Elite,* which he had written the year before, "The Cultural Apparatus" is defined by the coordination of the political, economic, and military institutions in American society. The power elite structures reality through its manipulation of master symbols. This is one of its means of legitimation.

National establishments tend to set the relations of culture and politics, the important tasks, the suitable themes, the major uses of the cultural apparatus. In the end, what is "established" are definitions of reality, judgments of value, canons of taste and beauty.[37]

All social structures are organized under the state. The state is in the business of power, and master symbols are used to perpetuate this power.

The social determinants of knowledge are therefore located by focusing upon the dominant institutional orders in a society. These institutional orders, through the manner in which they are integrated, define reality for those individuals who live out their lives in the particular society.

The cultural apparatus stands between consciousness and experience, perpetuating a false consciousness upon the individual.

The Sociological Imagination accepts this same analysis of American society, differing only in that Mills ascribes to the possessor of the sociological imagination an ability to dispel the false consciousness defined by the cultural apparatus. The sociologist must transcend the milieu in which he lives, and in order to do this he has to possess an understanding of the interrelations of the nature of man and the nature of society. Herein, Mills offers a sociology where action is entwined with analysis.

Mills thus comes full circle in the sociology of knowledge, answering his own call for a notion of social structure to firm up the amorphous conceptions of the pragmatists. This notion of social structure is, of course, his working model of a social system. "The Cultural Apparatus" and *The Sociological Imagination* take as implicit the assumption that American society is integrated around the mechanism of *coordination.* In the sociology of knowledge, as in all of his endeavors, Mills is attempting to synthesize social behaviorism and social structure.

The conditions that determine truth are defined by the mode of institutional integration present in any given society. Verification models are ultimately political. The sociology of knowledge as envisioned by Mills assails the absolute character of scientific truth by questioning its validation. Truth, to Dewey, is intrinsically tied to method; for Mills the sociology of knowledge studies the manner in which method becomes institutionalized. Rather than dealing with error as did Mannheim, Marx, and most other sociologists of knowledge, Mills is concerned with the integration of institutional frameworks—essential for any understanding of how world views are constructed. Unlike Mannheim, who was uneasy with relativism, Mills begins with relativism and analyzes how "relative truth" becomes institutionalized. Truth is not truth because it is pragmatic, as Mannheim said, but pragmatism is truth because it has been legitimized. Epistemological considerations are ultimately translated into political concerns.

6

SOCIAL STRATIFICATION: OCCUPATION, CLASS, STATUS, POWER, AND POWERLESSNESS

Stratification replaced the sociology of knowledge as Mills's major concern once he left graduate school. *The New Men of Power* (1948), *White Collar* (1951), and *The Power Elite* (1956) are Mills's major works in this area and represent various stages in his continuing effort to combine social behaviorism and Weberian sociology with a radical political orientation.

Basically, Mills's theory of stratification derives from Weber's famous class, status, and party (or power) trichotomy. Mills merely adds the dimension "occupation," defining it as follows:

By an occupation we understand a set of activities pursued more or less regularly as a major source of income.

From the individual's standpoint, occupational activities refer to types of skills that are marketable. As specific activities, occupations thus (1) entail various types and levels of skill, and (2) their exercise fulfills certain functions within an industrial division of labor....

As sources of income, occupations are thus connected with *class* position. Since occupations also normally carry an expected quota of prestige, on and off the job, they are relevant to *status* position. They also involve certain degrees of *power* over other people directly in terms of the job, and indirectly in other social areas.[1]

Class, or class situation, is related to the amount and source of income; "a class is a set of people who share similar life choices because of their similar class situations."[2] Mills's emphasis is always upon the unequal chances that accompany the various class situations.

Status or prestige requires more than one person; someone must claim the prestige and someone must honor the claim.

Power is obviously the most important dimension of stratification—for those who possess power can assert their will over others. For the most part, when we speak of power, political power is assumed; the social structure is organized under the political state.

Like Weber, Mills calls for an understanding of class in terms of probabilities based on objectively defined situations.

Class, status, power, and occupation form Mills's social-psychological theory of stratification. If individuals occupy similar strata they can be expected to manifest similar psychological traits even though their individual biographies might differ somewhat. Psychological factors are likely, too, to be associated with a particular stratum because the four dimensions intersect each other. By paying attention to this intersection traits can be systematically defined.

The four dimensions of stratification are simply ways of singling out certain features of specific roles in the various institutional orders; they provide the basis for understanding the social psychology of the various strata within a particular society. Mills's general model is implicit in all of his writings on stratification because he constantly reverts back to the relationship of different individuals to roles and institutional orders within American society. He offers two schemes of analysis, institutional orders and social strata, and uses them to look at the intricate range of possible relations that exist among the dimensions of stratification and the institutional orders that form any society.

STRATIFICATION: THREE PERIODS

Mills's writings on stratification can be divided into three distinct periods, all of which relate to the common theme of power as the most important dimension of stratification. The first period consists of the articles Mills wrote from 1942 to 1945; it represents Mills's search to locate the source of power in American society. Out of these articles would evolve the version of power later offered in *The Power Elite* (1956). These early 1940's articles (with two notable exceptions) were published in nonacademic radical and leftist journals[3] and represent what involvement Mills had in the radical intellectual circles of the time. After a brief sojourn at the University of Maryland, Mills had come to Columbia University to head the labor research division of the Bureau of Applied Social Research. Although Mills was physically close to the New York radical socialist cirlces, he never really was intellectually close to them. Born a Catholic, raised in the outlands of Texas, Mills had "profound feelings of uneasiness in confronting dyed-in-the-wool intellectuals, particularly Jewish intellectuals who made him feel the outsider."[4] This along with his history of being a loner made Mills at best only sympathetic to the Marxists of the 1940's.

As World War II wore on, Mills came more and more to see a basic similarity between Nazi Germany and the United States of the time. This becomes evident in his writings as he zeroes in on the interrelationship of monopoly capitalism and the state. As early as 1943 Mills begins to include the military as a partner in the triumvirate he envisions as controlling the United States. At this time Mills still held the belief that labor constituted the only major social power upon which a democracy could rest.[5] Mills would slowly lose this optimism for labor and by the late 1950's would completely reject any positive role for labor, referring instead to a "labor metaphysic."[6] The intellectual, in Mills's eyes, would come to replace labor as the historical agent for change.

In short then, two basic themes are interwoven in Mills's writings from 1942 to 1945: (1) his search for the locus of power in American society; and (2) the eventual eroding of a belief in the ability of the working class, specifically labor unions, to effect change, and the subsequent substitution of the intellectual as this agent.

In the second period, roughly from 1946 to the early 1950's, Mills was concerned not so much with power, but with powerlessness. *The New Men of Power* articulates the inability of the labor leader to assert power; *White Collar* describes the essential powerlessness of the middle class. We can see in the second period, too, a certain ambiguity in Mills's works, an ambiguity that comes out of the struggle with his fundamental "faith in intellectual activity as a basic way out of the morass of power"[7] and the day-to-day disillusionments he experienced as American society began to take on more and more of the totalitarian and bureaucratic tendencies that Weber had so vividly described. There is in *The New Men of Power* a striking example of this: Mills, who had all but given up any optimism for labor, nevertheless advocates a radical program of guild socialism. This program, stated in the form of the position of the left, calls for "a society in which everyone affected by a social decision, regardless of its sphere, would have a voice in the decision and a hand in its administration."[8] This would take the form of the establishing of workers' control over the social process of work through a political program held together by trade associations.

There is a certain sadness then, in *The New Men of Power;* Mills states the possibilities of labor radicalism—if such and such were to happen, *then* such and such would have to take place—while not forecasting or even treating his "if then" as likely to occur.[9] Even his call for a union of the power and the intellect, the possibility that labor leaders and intellectuals would get together and stop the drift toward a permanent war economy, is strained, because near the end of the book Mills dismisses the labor leaders by concluding that never has "so much depended upon men who are so ill-prepared and so little inclined to assume the responsibility."[10] Power lay elsewhere, and Mills grudgingly begins to admit this in *The New Men of Power.*

White Collar, Mills's major work of the early 1950's, extends the analysis of the reciprocal variables of power and powerlessness begun in *The New Men of Power,* especially how these variables shape social types. Power did not reside with either labor or the middle class—it lay somewhere else. The somewhere else was of course the power elite.

The New Men of Power and *White Collar,* which I will focus upon for period two, as well as *The Power Elite,* are therefore points on a continuum representing various stages in the development of Mills's thinking from the 1940's to the 1950's. In *The New Men of Power,* Mills's working model approach is still very much in the planning stage. It was more developed in *White Collar* and was completed by the time of period three, when he wrote *The Power Elite.* Because *The Power Elite* represents a theory based upon the completed model, as well as being Mills's most controversial work, a whole chapter will be devoted to it and to this third period.

These three works are thus related to the model in that they all represent a study of the psychological basis of stratification, Mills's search for the link between the "subjective" or "psychological" and the "objective" or "sociological."[11]

In order to introduce a specific analysis of Mills's writings in the periods under scrutiny, certain preliminary statements must be made. First of all, it should be stated that *The Puerto Rican Journey* (1950) does not fit into my scheme of analysis. The reasons for this are that (1) it was written in collaboration with two other authors, and even though Mills was the senior author it does not bear his distinctive stamp; and (2) it is primarily a methodological study of Puerto Rican immigrants, offering little in the way of a theoretical framework.[12]

Secondly, while *The New Men of Power* is ostensibly also a methodological study and, like *The Puerto Rican Journey,* grew out of Mills's affiliation with the Bureau of Applied Social Research, Mills was able to introduce theoretical issues into it. I do not claim that this is the most important part of *The New Men of Power;* nevertheless, the beginnings of a social psychology of stratification can be seen in it.

Third, and last, because it would fit in with his overall view of the structural changes in American society, Mills added the dimension of "occupation" to Weber's scheme of stratification. It was Mills's opinion that the most decisive shift in the twentieth century had been the decline of the independent entrepreneur, the "old middle class" as he labelled this group of small businessmen, farmers, and free professionals, and the subsequent rise of the "new middle class" comprising managers, office workers, and salaried professionals. The bureaucratization of Western civilization that Weber had foreseen had centralized property ownership, producing a shift from independent property holding to dependent job holding. The rise of the joint-stock company that Marx had analyzed had not, according to Mills, resulted in any real separation of ownership and control, nor had it contributed to the rise of a managerial class.[13] What had occurred though, was an attack on the democratic system—for control over the property one worked was indispensable for political freedom. *White Collar* deals with these structural changes, specifically with how these changes had produced this "new middle class." The middle class had become a society of employees, with occupation and occupational changes a key variable for an understanding of why this was so.

PERIOD I: MILLS'S EARLY FORMULATIONS CONCERNING POWER

For Mills, who had been a political innocent in the 1930's, World War II was a radicalizing experience. Indeed, it is more than likely that it was this innocence that made Mills more of a radical than a Marxist.[14] This would explain, too, the fact that Mills, although sympathetic to Marxism,[15] formulated an essentially non-Marxist analysis of power. In some of Mills's early articles we can see very clearly how he rejects basic Marxist tenets in favor of his own brand of radicalism. For instance, in an article written with Hans Gerth, "A Marx for the Managers" (1942), Gerth and Mills argue that economic power is always subordinate to political and legal regulation.[16] In what was essentially a critique of James Burnham's "managerial revolution" thesis, they also take Burnham to task for suffering from "too much Marx," dismissing his views in the following passage:

Burnham's theory of historical change does not take adequately into account the *de facto* functioning of class structures. For him the constituents of society are masses and elites. History is now a struggle between managers and weak, because functionally "superfluous," capitalists; later it will be between different managers, who will curb the masses with myths. In order to become dominant, all the managers must do is control the functional economy, silently knock over the remaining capitalists and curb the masses. This is all they have to do![17]

Gerth and Mills clearly choose Weber over Marx. Occupational skills are not identical with one's class position, nor with power, as Burnham implies. Mills makes virtually the same criticism in a 1942 review of W. Lloyd Warner and Paul Lunt's famous study of class, *The Social Life of a Modern*

Community. Warner and Lunt's use of the term *class* was inadequate because it absorbed such fundamentally different concepts as class, status, and power.[18]

Mills clearly never accepts a Marxian framework. He offers instead his own general framework, his working model of a social system. And the beginnings of the model, at least the social structure part, can be seen in "Collectivism and the Mixed-Up Economy," another article published in 1942. Here Mills argues that the United States is a political economy, that business and government are becoming intertwined. It was only a short step to the inclusion of the military, and Mills took this step a few months later in a review of Franz Neumann's book, *Behemoth: The Structure and Practice of National Socialism.* Here Mills focuses upon Neumann's position that four strategic elites dominated Nazi Germany: the monopoly capitalists, the Nazi party, the state bureaucracy, and the armed forces. Neumann's Germany was characterized by a specific type of capitalism, one he called "totalitarian monopolistic capitalism." Those who denied that Nazi Germany was capitalistic were, according to Mills, working under an erroneous conception of Marx's that capitalism is an anarchy of production. At the end of his review we can see that Mills was beginning to look at the United States in terms of its also being a "Behemoth." He writes:

That is why Franz Neumann's book is not only the most important to appear about Germany; it is a large contribution to all leftwing thinking today. His book will move all of us into deeper levels of analysis and strategy. It had better. Behemoth is everywhere united.[19]

In a review of Robert Brady's *Business as a System of Power,* Mills is even more explicit about the parallels in Roosevelt's America and Hitler's Germany: "There are structural trends in the political economy of the United States which parallel those of Germany."[20] Mills generally accepts Brady's theory that fascisim is linked to monopoly capitalism, infused with the state and implemented by the army. The United States, although not fascist, was heading that way. At this time Mills was still optimistic about labor's ability to stop this trend, and called for labor unions to unify into an independent political movement to take action on political issues. This optimism was soon eroded, and by the end of the war Mills's pessimism about labor was becoming fairly obvious. In "The Conscription of America," where Mills argues against peace-time conscription, he expresses the belief that America is heading toward a permanent war economy, a situation dependent on the cooperation of labor.

Faced with the thought of the eventual co-optation of labor, Mills turned at this time to the intellectual for a way out of the maze of powerlessness. In a 1944 article, "Intellectuals: The Powerless People," Mills tried to define the social situation of the intellectual. The intellectual wants desperately to have his thought matter, but the actuality of the situation renders him politically irrelevant. The intellectual, like labor leaders, salaried workers, indeed everyone but a few individuals at the center of power,[21] is separated from the realization of the consequences of his decisions. Action, for the intellectual, is removed from thought. Though he envisioned the intellectual as powerless, Mills refused to see the situation as hopeless. The reasons for the ineffectualness of the intellectual can be traced to a political failure of nerve. The intellectual assumes the role of "detached spectator" and blames his inaction on insufficient knowledge. Political action is the answer. For "the political man is always aware that while events are not in his hands he must bear their consequences."[22] Mere understanding is not enough.

The political man does not need to wait upon more knowledge in order to act responsibly now. To blame his inaction upon insufficient knowledge serves as a cheap escape from the taking of a political stand and acting upon it as best he can. If one half of the relevant knowledge which we now possess were really put into the service of the ideals which leaders mouth, these ideals could be realized in short order. The view that all that is needed is knowledge ignores the nub of the problem as the social scientist confronts it: he has little or no power to act politically and his chance to communicate in a politically effective manner is very limited.[23]

The intellectual must locate himself within his social structure and then formulate a political strategy. Mills, though he does not offer a specific strategy in this article, does end on a note of optimism, something notably lacking in his other works. He expresses the belief that "problems are really going to be solved in his [the intellectual's] medium, that of the word."[24] He would of course take up this theme again in such articles as "The Decline of the Left" (1959), "Culture and Politics" (1959), and "The New Left" (1960), as well as in *The Sociological Imagination* (1959).

Mills's early writings in the 1940's represent an attempt to locate the basis of power in American society. In them we can see Mills's initial encounter with Marxism and the beginnings of a non-Marxist analysis of power which would culminate in his working model and his power elite theory. Running throughout these early articles are a waning of enthusiasm for labor and a subsequent substitution of the intellectual as the most viable agent of change. This emphasis upon the political intellectual to effect change goes back to Mills's training in pragmatism, with its emphasis upon action as well as theory.

PERIOD II: "THE NEW MEN OF POWER" AND "WHITE COLLAR"

"The New Men of Power"

The New Men of Power is a description of the origins of the union leader and his role as a new elite. By focusing on the rise of the labor leader, Mills also provides an analysis of the evolution of the working class.

In *The New Men of Power* Mills concentrates upon the dimension of power, along with its intersection with the other dimensions of stratification showing how a particular type of role, that of the labor leader, is produced. Due to their similarity in occupation, class, status, and power, labor leaders can be expected to manifest a sameness of personality. On the other hand, given that their income, or class, is not high, an important distinction between them and other elites of power emerges. What we have then is an attempt by Mills to relate a "type" of social role to a particular social structure. By focusing upon Mills's conception of social structure we can look at the interrelationship of the labor leader's character traits and the social milieu in which he acts out his role.

First of all, Mills sees the shift away from the large-scale ownership of private property to dependent job holding as the most important economic factor of mid-twentieth-century America. The growth of trade unions is part of this same shift. Without such a change there would be no need for labor unions.

The labor leader is thereby in a unique position. He is not of the elite of class or prestige but of the elite of power. Power lies within the institution. The labor leader wields power by virtue of his position in the union. How does this power and the other dimensions of stratification affect him? To answer this question Mills studies five hundred labor leaders, a representative cross section of American society's national, state, and city labor leaders, and analyzes how the institutions they belong to help form their social characteristics. This is what Mills would also do, although in slightly different form, in *White Collar* and *The Power Elite.* He is interested not in the labor leader as an individual but as a type—a type formed by the social roles played within the economic institutional order. In order to understand the labor leader one had to understand the labor union and its role in American society; one also had to understand the sometimes curious role the labor leader played in interaction with the businessmen and politicians encountered in the economic order.

As in *Sociology and Pragmatism,* Mills is also concerned with the relationship of the labor leader to his publics. Two types of public are singled out for special consideration. One Mills labels the "liberal center," the other, the "sophisticated conservatives." The former most often support the policies of the unions; the latter are occupants of the trade association world. There was another public, that of the American mass society, but Mills dismissed it as politically passive.

The sophisticated conservatives represent the genesis of the power elite. The beginnings of Mills's famous theory are readily apparent in the following passage:

The sophisticated right . . . tie in solidly with the industry-armed forces-State Department axis, and move personally as well as politically in those circles. The interchange between the military and big industry is more wide spread and easier than most observers realize; intermarriages, as well as explicit career moves, would have to be taken into account in any thorough study of these connections. Since this tiny political group is not at present attempting directly to enlist public support, the terms of its real ideology are not well known. Probably as they see it, the high military and the big management should unite and form a new elite.[25]

Mills envisions the politics of the time as an engagement between the "sophisticated conservatives" and the "liberal center," with the former getting the upper hand. This was the reason why the labor leader was so important, why Mills devoted a book to him.

The labor leaders are thus tied to the structural or institutional changes occurring within American society. The sophisticated conservatives align themselves with the military, and America heads toward a social structure integrated through the process of coordination. The labor leaders are caught between this "drift," as Mills calls it, and the oncoming of a mass society. How the labor leaders would act in the face of these trends was the key question anyone interested in American society at mid-century had to ask. And Mills's answer lay in the social and psychological variables shaping the actions of the labor leaders.

Bureaucracy, the separateness (at that time) of the AFL and CIO, the differences in the ages and education of the leaders of the two branches, the fact that most labor leaders were self-made men—all had to be taken into consideration. In particular, the self-made man syndrome was extremely important, because self-made men tend to look down upon those who do not make it. A conflict arises when the labor leader, who although professing a pro-working man ideology, increases his salary, changes his style of life, gains prestige, and thereby goes beyond the realm of his original reference group. These changes particularly affect his political behavior. The union leader begins to embrace the liberal rhetoric, the key words of which are *cooperation, good will,* and *intelligence.* If only men of both sides manifested good will and showed intelligence in their dealings with one another there would be no conflict between the interests of the working class and management—or so states the rhetoric.

This cooperation implies a mutual goal for business and labor—to profit economically. The ones who suffer and bear the brunt of the cooperation are, of course, the consumers. Dead set against this form of collusion, Mills sees it as leading the United States into a corporate form of the garrison state. The labor leader thus does nothing to halt what Mills considers to be the coming establishment of a permanent war economy. In order to do this the union leader would have had to try to organize the white-collar workers into a coalition with the working class. Together they might stop this drift toward slump and a permanent war economy.

As has been stated a number of times, Mills would later abandon any hope that the labor leader would be able to stop the drift toward coordination. In *White Collar*, as we shall see, Mills portrays the middle classes as alienated and lacking political consciousness. In *The Power Elite* he describes a social system in which the "sophisticated conservatives," the military, and the political leadership are shaped by coordination. *The New Men of Power*, *White Collar*, and *The Power Elite* represent a trilogy of sorts. All three deal with the relationships of particular strata to the institutional changes in American society.

What Mills shows in *The New Men of Power* is this: the labor leaders, by virtue of their occupation and the prestige attached to their position, are thrust into positions of power. "The power position of institutions and individuals typically depends upon factors of class, status, and occupation, often in intricate interrelation."[26]

The structural changes in American society, the shift from independent property owning to dependent job holding, place the labor leaders in key positions. Mills's pragmatic training becomes apparent when he calls for action in terms of an alliance of the labor leaders with intellectuals and the "new middle class." Only through such an alliance can a solution to the problem of the drift to slump be found. Mills, although pessimistic, is quite emphatic in this call for action.

As in much of Mills's writing, his work suffers when he introduces the normative. This, along with the fact that Mills does not accomplish what he sets out to do, is a basic weakness in *The New Men of Power*. Mills attempts to portray the labor leader as a social type, to focus upon the roles he plays within society and how the society shaped these roles; but what we get instead is a collective portrait of five hundred labor leaders, with only the variables of age and education broken down for us, and only then to distinguish between AFL and CIO leaders. Mills's hope of combining the qualitative with the quantitative falls short because his frame of reference is inadequate. He had not as yet fully integrated his pragmatic training with a viable notion of social structure; therefore *The New Men of Power* is without any real mechanism for analyzing the types of individuals formed by their social structure. The point that should be emphasized here is that Mills would later come to stress that individuals are formed by institutions, not by society. They are socialized, seek rewards, internalize defined values, desire goals, and act in compliance with institutions. The same criticism Mills raises concerning George Herbert Mead's concept of the "generalized other" can be levelled against him here. Between the individual and his society lie intermediary agencies of socialization. Only when Mills works this out in terms of his general model of a social system do his works begin to take on an internal consistency. A fundamental weakness in *The New Men of Power*, then, is that although Mills mentions institutional orders, his emphasis centers on relating the individual to his society through such intermediaries as publics or images held of the labor leader. Mills does not offer an adequate social psychology; instead there is a mixture of pragmatism and some Weberian analysis, with the end result that *The New Men of Power* is more important as a genesis of later ideas than for any realization of the concepts introduced within its pages. The same cannot be said of *White Collar*, where Mills's working model is more fully developed.

"White Collar": The American Middle Classes

"The Middle Classes in Middle Sized Cities" is a preliminary statement of what Mills would elaborate in *White Collar*. In it he reiterates the belief that certain psychological traits recur among individuals of the same strata. Mills's argument is based on his belief that "the probability that people will have a similar mentality and ideology, and that they will join together for action, is increased the more homogeneous they are with respect to class, occupation, and prestige."[27]

In "Middle Classes," Mills is concerned with this homogeneity, particularly as it affects political consciousness. The white-collar worker and the small businessman are analyzed to see whether or not each of them constitutes a homogeneous stratum, whether or not they display any political consciousness. In this empirical study Mills finds that any political ideology held by the white-collar individual arises directly out of his occupation and is invoked primarily to set up social distinctions between him and labor. Political organization and political awareness are at a minimum. The white-collar workers in these middle-class cities are divorced from any organization of power.[28] *White Collar* elaborates on these findings.

In *White Collar*, as the subtitle states, Mills is interested in the middle class in American society and uses the beginnings of his working model approach to understand this class. In his introduction to *White Collar*, he states:

We need to characterize American society of the mid-twentieth century in more psychological terms, for now the problems that concern us most border on the psychiatric. It is one great task of social studies today to describe the larger economic and political situation in terms of its meaning for the inner life and the external career of the individual, and in doing this to take into account how the individual often becomes falsely conscious and blinded. In the welter of the individual's daily experience the framework of modern society must be sought; within that framework the psychology of the little man must be formulated.

The first lesson of modern sociology is that the individual cannot understand his own experience or gauge his own fate without locating himself within the trends of his epoch and the life-chances of all the individuals of his social layer. To understand the white-collar people in detail, it is necessary to draw at least a rough sketch of the social structure of which they are a part. For the character of any stratum consists in large part of its relations, or lack of them, with the strata above and below it; its peculiarities can best be defined by noting its differences from other strata. The situation of the new middle class, reflecting conditions and styles of life that are borne by elements of both the new lower and new upper classes, may be seen as symptom and symbol of modern society as a whole.[29]

The similarity to what Mills would later call the "sociological imagination" is apparent in the above quotation. Mills, therefore, uses his model to analyze the massive changes that had taken place in the class structure of the United States since the nineteenth century. All the sociologist had to do to locate these changes was look at the related consequences of these changes upon the social roles of the individual. To understand the middle class, one had to sketch the relation of the character of the white-collar worker to the changing institutions. In *White Collar,* Mills discerns the typical motivations required by individuals as necessary and sufficient for the enactment of these roles and shows how the central ideas and beliefs of a society, its communication and symbols, contribute to the formation, maintenance, and effectiveness of these motivations.

White Collar is a social-psychological study of how the bureaucratization of the economic institutional order affects the social biographies of those individuals who act out social roles within this order. The best way to focus on this is to use the four dimensions of stratification and apply them to an analysis of the middle class, and the bureaucratization that shapes the lives of those who make up this strata.

Occupation.   The shift in occupation must be traced to its historical roots. According to Mills, "unlike the European, the American middle class enters modern history as a big stratum of small entrepreneurs."[30] Europe was characterized by a peasant mass, while America had a scattering of farmers. This was the basic difference in the social structure of the two.

Prior to the Civil War, farmers and small businessmen constituted a large part of the middle class. "The industrialization of America, especially after the Civil War, gave rise not to a broad stratum of small businessmen, but to the captain of industry. He was our first national image of the middle class man as businessman, and no one has ever supplanted him."[31] The most important characteristic of the middle class at the time was that they owned the property with which they worked. The rich were so few as to be almost inconsequential. In relation to the institutional shaping of character, the emerging social type was an individualist. Because biography, history, and social structure are so intimately entwined, a change in one produces change in the others. The old middle class began to disappear as the society became more and more bureaucratized.

In the twentieth century, technology continued rapidly to expand; but the expansion of the market took place much more slowly. In the attempt to stabilize matters, the captains of industry began to draw together and out of their epic competition there emerged impersonal monopoly. . . . As the concentration of private enterprise began to change the type of businessman that prevailed, the Captain of Industry gave way to the Rentier, the Absentee Owner, the Corporation Executive and . . . the New Entrepreneur.[32]

The major occupational shifts followed the industrial trend; workers ceased to make things. They began more and more to handle people and symbols. It could be no other way in a bureaucratized society.

Class.   One's class is defined by one's amount and source of income. In America, occupation has replaced property as the source of income for the middle class. Mills holds that "the possibilities of selling their services in the labor market, rather than of profitably buying and selling their property and its yields, . . . determine the life chances of most of the middle class."[33] No longer could the worker receive any personal satisfaction from his labor; money is the only significant criterion. However, it is an economic fact of life that the white-collar worker does not receive much more in income than his lower-class counterpart. Labor unions enable the lower-class individual to almost approximate the class position of the white-collar worker. They are both in the same propertyless class situation; neither has any tie to production. The differences between the middle and lower classes are to be found somewhere else.

Status.   Although mass production has lessened many of the distinctions between the white-collar worker and the wage worker, some, nevertheless, still remain. Status or prestige claims require the honoring by others, and in the long run also require widely acknowledged bases which distinguish one stratum from those above or below. White-collar workers try to compensate for what Mills labels "the status panic" by borrowing prestige. One manner of borrowing occurs when the white-collar worker comes in contact with those of higher status and simply uses this access to borrow prestige. The outstanding example of this is the salesgirl on Fifth Avenue who looks down on her counterpart in other neighborhoods. Another way is to borrow prestige from the large organization one works for. All told, however, the major way to prestige for the white-collar worker is through education. Education, for the middle class, replaces property as the primary means of achieving social position. Here is an example of where a sphere (education) reinforces the institutional orders and is even used as a means of social control. The meaning of education shifts along with the changes in American society, and its primary function now lies with the occupational and economic areas. Education is the key to success, perhaps the only means to success. But in the Millsian scheme of analysis, this success is of a limited variety.

Power. Power, the fourth dimension of stratification, is always the most important one. Reinforcing his conclusions in "Middle Classes," Mills calls attention to the powerlessness of the middle classes. Hinting at trends he would explore more fully in *The Power Elite*, Mills envisions power becoming more and more concentrated at the top.

Changes have occurred within the industrial propertied class in such a way that the actual wielding of power is delegated to hierarchies; the entrepreneurial function has been bureaucratized. But the top man in the bureaucracy is a powerful member of the propertied class. He derives his right to act from the institution of property; he does act in so far as he possibly can in a manner he believes is to the interests of the private-property system; he does feel in unity, politically and status-wise as well as economically, with his class and its source of wealth.[34]

Power has shifted to the large institutions within the society, and the forms of power wielded represent a shift from explicit authority to manipulation. Not only does the large bureaucratic organization manifest this shift, but so too does the symbol sphere through the means of mass communication. The result is a departure from the nineteenth-century system of explicit authority to the modern epoch, where the individual is manipulated without knowing it. Organized irresponsibility is a leading characteristic of modern industrial society.

With power resting within the hierarchies of large-scale bureaucracies the individual is stripped of any control over his work and, by extension, his life. "The Cheerful Robot" that Mills would elaborate upon in *The Sociological Imagination,* springs into existence. The individual is forced to seek what little satisfaction is open to him off the job. The state of the white-collar worker is one of alienation—his politics that of the powerless. The distance between the individual and the centers of power is greater and greater, and the individual begins to feel more and more powerless. The new middle class is a stratum of followers of power, not a balancing factor upon which conditions of democratic stability depend.

Roles and Institutional Orders.   The four dimensions of stratification are concepts that enable the sociologist to focus upon particular roles in various institutional orders. This was always one of Mills's primary concerns. *White Collar* deals with the relationships between biography and social structure, or the type of personality that is produced by the changes Mills saw American society going through. The methodology involved is that of the "rational caricature,"[35] the ideal type role formed within an institutional context. One example given by Mills is that of the executives who make up what he calls the "managerial demiurge." The executives follow clearly defined, interrelated lines of authority. Their power is located in the office they hold and is clearly demarcated; their relations are impersonal and set by the hierarchical structure. Even their expectations are thoroughly calculable. Of another social type are the "new professionals," who, like most of the white-collar workers, are becoming more and more attached to a large bureaucracy with an attendant effect upon their social roles and personalities. Mills also dissects the social type he knows best, the academic. Drawing an analogy between the economic institutional order and the educational sphere, Mills comes up with the following subtypes:

The *producer* is the man who creates ideas, first sets them forth, or at any rate makes them available in writing to those portions of the market capable of understanding them. . . . Then there are the *wholesalers,* who while they do not produce ideas, do distribute them in textbooks to other academic men, who in turn sell them directly to student consumers. In so far as men teach, and only teach they are *retailers* of ideas and materials, the better of them being serviced by original producers, the lesser, by wholesalers. All academic men, regardless of type, are also *consumers* of the products of others, of producers and wholesalers through books, and of retailers to some extent through personal conversation and local markets. But it is possible for some to specialize in consumption: these become great *comprehenders,* rather than users, of books, and they are great on bibliographies.[36]

The academic is the equivalent of the new entrepreneur. The professorial entrepreneur is an academic who is capable of furthering his career in the university by securing power and prestige outside its confines. He is the one who sets up or runs the financed institute which puts the university in contact with those individuals who are in the top echelons of the white-collar society.

Mills reverts briefly in his portrait of the academic entrepreneur to a sociology of knowledge analysis. His thesis is that the growth of this new type of professor has pushed the academician closer to the technician, and in so doing strengthens an apolitical professional ideology.

Perhaps Mills's greatest contribution in *White Collar* is his description of the world of the salesman, for as Mills so aptly puts it, the world of the salesman has "become everybody's world, and in some part, everybody has become a salesman."[37] Selling replaces production as the most important economic function in American society. The primary concern of the American economy is selling—not anything in particular, but just selling. Changes in the social structure produce changes in social roles and the social types who make up what Mills refers to as "The Great Salesroom." Salesgirls are divided into such types as "The Wolf"; "The Charmer"; "The Ingenue Salesgirl"; "The Collegiate"; "The Drifter"; "The Social Pretender"; and "The Old Timer."

As for the salesman: "Since the first decade of the century, much bureaucratic attention has been given to the gap between mass production and individual consumption. Salesmanship is an attempt to fill that gap."[38] In selling, as everywhere, institutionalization, rationalization, and centralization produce "the appropriation of certain traits previously found in creative salesmen, by a machinery that codifies these traits and controls their acquisition and display by individual salesmen."[39]

Selling is to be understood in terms of the "personality market," which comes out of the shift from manual skills to those skills required in the handling of people.

From the salesman and the personality market Mills turns to the white-collar office worker and his world of "the enormous file." What social roles do those who work in the enormous file play? How does their character relate to the social structure in which they live out their biographies? Theirs is essentially a world of alienation from their work.

The objective alienation of man from the product and the process of work is entailed by the legal framework of modern capitalism and the modern division of labor. The worker does not own the product or the tools of his production. In the labor contract he sells his time, energy, and skill into the power of others. . . . In all work involving the personality market . . . one's personality traits become part of the means of production. In this sense a person instrumentalizes and externalizes intimate features of his person and dispositions. In certain white-collar areas, the rise of personality markets has carried self and social alienation to explicit extremes.[40]

White-collar workers are not free within the economic institution, and this lack of freedom becomes more and more a dominant trait in their character structure as they habitually submit to the wills of others. Their only hope lies in their attempt to build a life outside the realm of work; their salvation rests with their leisure time.

This is the portrait of the white-collar worker as painted by C. Wright Mills. It is a bleak, discouraging picture of the effects of rationalization and bureaucracy upon the economic institutional order. The individual in Mills's scheme is trapped by the drift of modern capitalism. There is no way out for him. The "new middle class" arose out of an occupational shift from independent entrepreneurs to white-collar workers. Class lines are blurred between blue-collar workers and white-collar workers. The general result is the formation of a powerless social type cast adrift in a society that is fast becoming a mass society. The "new middle class," like the labor leaders, defaults in the struggle for power. The locus of power resides in the hierarchies of large-scale institutions. The inheritance of the white-collar worker is a world of alienation from power, from work, and from self.

The United States is characterized by political indifference. The Marxian notion of class consciousness is lacking among those of the middle stratum. In order to have class consciousness, three things are necessary: "(1) a rational awareness and identification with one's own class interests; (2) an awareness of and rejection of other class interests as illegitimate; and (3) an awareness of and a readiness to use collective political means to the collective political end of realizing one's interests."[41] These elements do not exist among the middle class. The middle class is so divorced from power that anxiety and insecurity are general psychological traits. The middle-class person is confused, unfocused, and discontinuous in his actions. He literally has nowhere to go. The white-collar worker is an alienated man, adrift in a bureaucratic world he never made. His alienation from his work in the economic order extends to the political order. The mass media reinforce this alienation, and the result is political indifference.

Men do "enter into definite, necessary relations which are independent of their will," but, communications enter to slant the meanings of these relations for those variously involved in them. The forms of political consciousness may, in the end, be relative to the means of production, but, in the beginning, they are relative to the contents of the communication media.[42]

In mass communication, formula replaces form. The mass media are the common denominator of the American experience, and it is an essentially empty experience.

White Collar paints a bleak picture of American society, and this may very well be a weakness in it. According to Mills, the individual is trapped, with no way out. Actually it is not this simple. In order to have the society Mills envisioned, America would have to be a total mass society. Nowhere did Mills say this was so. He always implies that America is on the way to, or drifting toward, a mass society. Another weakness, as David Riesman pointed out in a review of *White Collar,* is that Mills does not discuss the ethnic coloring of attitudes toward the middle class.[43] By this Riesman means that Mills fails to recognize, or at least overlooks, the fact that for certain ethnic groups, ascent into the middle class is considered a plus. This is particularly true of urban working-class Irish and Italian Catholics, for whom ascent into the middle class is almost synonymous with "making it" in American society."[44]

On balance, however, *White Collar* is a fine book—in the opinion of many, Mills's finest.[45] The reason for this is that in *White Collar* Mills begins to put together his synthesis of pragmatism and Weberian sociology. The Weberian notion of the bureaucratization of society is imposed upon the personality structure of those who live and work within the large-scale institutions. Mills analyzes the structural changes in American society and their impact upon the psychology of the individuals in that society and gives us an analysis based on the beginnings of a working model of a social system. The result is one of the finest dissections of the middle class written by an American sociologist. Mills is well on his way to his synthesis.

7

POWER: PERIOD III

The Power Elite is an application of Mills's working model of a social system—a social-psychological theory of stratification drawn in terms of the institutional integration of society. Implicit in this theory is an intricate elaboration of Mills's three-part conception of power as coercion, authority, and manipulation.[1] Power is defined by Mills in the Weberian sense—it is the ability to realize one's will even if others resist it.[2] Power is but one dimension of stratification (the most important one, to be sure) and is always found with occupation, class, and status. Power is cumulative, and *The Power Elite,* like *White Collar* and to a lesser extent *The New Men of Power,* is a study of social types—an attempt to relate the psychological characteristics of the individual to his social structure by stratification theory.

Careful to avoid the economic concept "ruling class," Mills instead opts for Weber, producing a more comprehensive study than the usual Marxist analysis. In Mills's scheme, power resides in institutions. America is integrated through an interlocking domination of the political, economic, and military institutional orders, with those who occupy the top positions in these orders in charge.

Mills is interested in two things in *The Power Elite:* (1) how American society at mid-century is integrated, and (2) how the individual is shaped by institutional orders in light of this integration. Mills's theory of stratification and his conception of power are the bridges that connect the individual to his society.

"THE POWER ELITE": A THEORY OF STRATIFICATION

The central theme of *The Power Elite* is the presence of a ruling stratum in America composed of "those political, economic, and military circles which as an intricate set of overlapping cliques shape decisions having at least national consequences. In so far as national events are decided, the power elite are those who decide them."[3] Three basic keys, the psychology of the several elites as manifested in their respective milieux, the structure and mechanics of the institutional hierarchies, and the integrative principle of coordination, are essential for an understanding of those who make up the power elite. The fundamental question asked is, what is the nature of the elite in each institutional order?

First, the economic order. Do the elite of the economic order, or as Mills refers to them, the corporate elite, form a distinctive social type? Do they perform and incorporate similar role experiences? Looking at the careers of five hundred of the top executives in 1950, Mills found that the executive career was almost entirely a career within the corporate world—that less than 10 percent of the top executives since 1920 entered their positions from independent professional or outside hierarchies. In order to become a member of the corporate elite an executive has to be well-liked, and an insider. He has to be an individual who fits in with those already at the top. One not only has to meet the expectations of his superiors, one has to imitate his superiors. Competence is judged by conformity to the values of those already at the top. "To be compatible with the top men is to act like them, to look like them, to think like them; to be of and for them—or at least to display oneself to them is such a way as to create that impression."[4]

In the economic order the cues are given by the corporate elite, and the "bright young boys" perform their proper roles within the institution. The end product is a similarity of personality types. As for the political institutions, Mills defines two major types of politicians: the political insider, who works through the party organization, and the Johnny-come-lately. The political elite comes from the second type, and as a group, the political outsiders (who occupy the executive command posts and form the political directorate) are legal, managerial, and financial members of the corporate rich. They are powerful Johnny-come-latelies with the same basic backgrounds. The dimensions of stratification intersect quite nicely in their case.

The military order also produces a sameness in those who ascend its hierarchy. "The harsh initiation at the Point or the Academy—and on the lower levels of the military service, in basic training—reveals the attempt to break up early civilian values and sensibilities in order to more easily implant a character structure."[5] They also have a similar experience, their early milieux having been wiped out. The result again is a sameness of character.

These elites with their institutionally shaped social personalities are related through the mechanism of coordination to the integration of American society. There are no longer a separate economy, an autonomous political order, and a subservient military order. Historical trends have linked the three.

The economy—once a great scatter of small productive units in autonomous balance—has become dominated by two or three hundred giant corporations, administratively and politically interrelated, which together hold the keys to economic decisions.

The political order, once a decentralized set of several dozen states with a weak spinal cord, has become a centralized, executive establishment which has taken up into itself many powers previously scattered, and now enters into each and every cranny of the social structure.

The military order, once a slim establishment in a context of distrust fed by state militia, has become the largest and most expensive feature of government, and, although well versed in smiling public relations, now has all the grim and clumsy efficiency of a sprawling bureaucratic domain.

In each of these institutional areas, the means of power at the disposal of decision makers have increased enormously; their central executive powers have been enhanced; within each of them modern administrative routines have been elaborated and tightened up.

As each of these domains becomes enlarged and centralized, the consequences of its activities become greater, and its traffic with others increases.[6]

As the institutions converge there is an overlapping of the men whose biographies are lived out within the milieux that make up the ruling clique. Their social origin and common education make them better able to understand and trust one another. As they continue to associate, a further bond develops and solidifies. Members of the higher circles in America thus become personal friends, perhaps even neighbors, as they meet each other both inside and outside the occupational domain.

The unity of this power elite consists in the ease of interchangeability within these three levels. The general becomes a board chairman, the corporation president a cabinet member. Cohesiveness, essential to an elitist interpretation, is produced by the principle of coordination. As coordination evolves, the two remaining institutions, the kinship and religious orders, work to reinforce the power elite through the educational sphere. The elitist private or "prep" school becomes a training ground for the socialization of upper-class youths. While not religious schools, they are permeated by religiously inspired principles that lend support to the status quo.

The kinship order, the religious order, and the educational sphere become increasingly decentralized and are shaped more and more by the three ascendant orders. Their main function, along with that of the other spheres, is reinforcement.

Symbols

The symbolic sphere reinforces and legitimizes the power structure via the mass media. The media tell the individual what he is, what he wants to be, how he should feel, and why all this is so. The propagandist, the publicity expert, the public relations men control public opinion and maintain the status quo. Manipulation is an instrument for preserving power, as the powerful seek to rule without publicized legitimation. The power elite use the mass media to convince the nation that power and authority reside in the people, when in reality anything but that occurs.

Technology and Status

Technology, because it is connected with the large-scale institution, lends strength to the process of coordination. The power elite works through the large-scale organization, and technology becomes the handmaiden of power.[7]

Status is envisioned in the same manner as it was in *White Collar.* Occupational shifts have located status in the positions at the top of large-scale institutions. Status, as always, follows power.

In sum, Mills's power elite is a ruling stratum in a society integrated through the coordination of the political, economic, and military institutions. The other two institutional orders and the five spheres reinforce this coordination. Due to the institutional shaping of individuals as well as the intersection of the four dimensions of stratification, the power elite constitutes a social type. The ruling strata manifest similar social-psychological traits. They hold power because they are in positions of authority within institutions and can manipulate via the symbol sphere. Since status follows power, those who are in positions of power accrue the most status. Those in the power elite are given similar status deferences; and since status is closely correlated with self-image, a sameness results here, too. Members of the power elite also manifest similarities in occupations. Given the bureaucratization of all large institutions, there is a basic compatibility between jobs, and a correspondence between positions in institutions—hence the easy transition from one top position to another. As for class, although it is anchored to the property institutions and occupational roles of the economic order, class considerations are also part of the political economy.

The power elite is fairly homogeneous with respect to power, class, occupation, and status. It follows that there is a high probability that those who make up this stratum will manifest a similar mentality and ideology, will possess a class consciousness. This, as Mills had already shown, is not attributable to the middle and lower classes. *The Power Elite* is an attempt to document this conception of the ruling elite in terms of individuals who perform similar social roles and are thereby similar social types. Mills followed *The Power Elite* with *The Causes of World War III* in 1958. Convinced that the power elite was leading the United States into a total and absurd war, he outlines a number of proposals to stop the thrust toward war. These proposals range from unilateral nuclear disarmament by America to the abandonment of all military bases and installations outside the United States. War is the enemy, and Mills, true to form, calls upon the intellectuals of both sides to make a separate peace.

Unfortunately there are many weaknesses among Mills's proposals, the most substantial being that Mills minimizes the differences between political ideology and leadership on both sides. While the East and West may be heading in the same direction, they are being pushed by very different forces.

Basically, though, because *Causes* is an extension of *The Power Elite*, its strength or weakness must rest upon the overall viability of Mills's ruling stratum thesis.

Up to this point I have not offered any criticism of *The Power Elite*, for in spite of all the criticism tendered against Mills's theory of power (some of which, particularly the nonideological, is well taken), I believe that Mills's general analysis is essentially correct. He may have erred on certain points, but his overall framework—his general working model—provides a better means for understanding the nature of power in American society than do other schemes. Mills's critics misunderstood him by failing to see the importance of his model as a heuristic device for analyzing American society. Mills's thesis of a power elite must be assessed in terms of his model and the basic question is whether or not the model can handle the major criticisms levelled at *The Power Elite*.

Criticisms of *The Power Elite* can roughly be divided into two kinds: those of a pluralistic or liberal bent and the radical or Marxist critiques.

PLURALISTIC CRITICISMS

Pluralistic criticisms of *The Power Elite* come under five basic headings: (1) Mills's failure to demonstrate a cohesion among members of the elite; (2) Mills's view that power is cumulative; (3) Mills's relegation of Congress and political parties to the middle level of power; (4) Mills's overemphasizing the power of the military; and (5) Mills's use of a sociology-of-leadership approach as opposed to a decision-making one.

Cohesion

In general, Mills's pluralistic critics believe that there is no elite whose interests are opposed to the masses of American society. Daniel Bell, one of Mills's most vocal critics, argues, for instance, that an elite community of interests is implied in *The Power Elite* but never proven.[8] Robert Dahl, perhaps political science's most prominent spokesman for pluralism, questions in another context whether such interests exist at all when it is well known that there is disagreement among America's leaders.[9] Neither Bell nor Dahl has looked at Mills's thesis in terms of his model. Mills's position is that institutions produce psychological and sociological similarities in individuals. Those who arrive at the top do so because they have internalized the necessary character traits. Socialization, not conspiracy, produces cohesion. As for a community of interests, why not the maintenance of the capitalistic system—the preservation of the status quo—and on an individual level, a consolidation of material and ideological personal states.[10] Such an assertion, as Mills points out, holds for every group. Isn't it logical that those who are in control should seek to preserve and possibly enhance the control and accruements which come with their power? Also, certain recent qualifications to Mills's power elite thesis offered by G. William Domhoff are worth noting. Domhoff writes:

In claiming that important national decisions are controlled by a power elite which has its roots in and serves the interests of the American upper class, several caveats must be added. The control is not complete; other groups sometimes have their innings, particularly when these groups are well organized and angry. Nor is the power elite always united in its policies; there are longstanding disagreements between its moderate and conservative wings on some issues, as manifested, for example in the arguments between the Committee for Economic Development and the National Association of Manufacturers. Nor does the power elite automatically act in its best interests; to read case studies of specific decisions is to be aware that lack of information, misunderstandings and personality clashes may lead to mistakes on issues that must be decided in a hurry.[11]

Mills himself writes that members of the power elite "are frequently in some tension: they come together only on certain points, and only on certain occasions of crisis."[12]

The Cumulativeness of Power

The argument against the cumulative nature of power implies that power does not necessarily correlate with other stratified resources. "Power is an empirically separable variable of social stratification,"[13] notes Nelson Polsby, a close associate of Dahl. The famous New Haven power studies are offered as proof of the separateness of power, status, and class. Polsby asks us to accept his position because he and his associates found that New Haven was a pluralistic democracy with power dispensed among various groups. The microcosm stands for the macrocosm, or so Polsby argues. Because of what is found in the university community of New Haven we are asked to believe that an individual who is at the top of the political, economic, or military institutional orders is not at the apex of authority, status, and wealth. To put it mildly, community power studies have little to do with national elite studies; to assert that they do, as the pluralists have done, leaves much to be desired as a logical practice.

The Relegation of Congress and Political Parties to Middle Levels of Power

Critics of the power elite theory argued in the late 1950's and early 1960's that Mills had overlooked the importance of elected officials. However, with the Vietnam War, by the late 1960's and early 1970's it became more and more apparent that the Congress of the United States was ineffectual and impotent in foreign affairs. And given Congress's recent gyrations as it sought to deal with Nixon and Watergate, and then its failure to develop an energy policy in the face of President Ford's vetoes, its impotence seems undeniable. The argument then shifts to the president, who is an elected official, and not necessarily a member of an elite.[14] But a close look at the argument reveals its inherent weakness. First of all, the president can only rise to the office if his thinking corresponds to the economic interests whose support is essential for financial backing in a long campaign. Secondly, before a president can receive the nomination of his party, he must have demonstrated over a long period of time that his views fit in with the prevailing views of the party. Third and last, the president usually depends to such an extent on his advisers (men, as Mills shows, who are recruited from the top positions in the economic, political, and military institutional orders) that these advisers in effect make the decisions.[15]

The Role of the Military

The one area upon which all of Mills's critics agreed concerns his view of the role of the military. A. A. Berle, Jr., in a review of *The Power Elite* entitled "Are the Blind Leading the Blind," can be taken as representative. Says Berle: Mills "is wrong in asserting a general 'coincidence of interest between military and corporate needs as defined by war lords and corporate rich'; and corporate capitalism is not a 'military capitalism,' save in a few specialized fields."[16] Here, I would have to agree slightly with Mills's detractors. It is almost as if Mills wrote two different versions of the role of the military. While the first is a fine description of the socialization process of America's "War Lords," as he dubbed them, the second never tells us quite how and why they are equal to the political and economic elites. In fairness to Mills, though, it must be pointed out that he never states that there is perfect cohesion between military and civilian interests. What he argues is that we are living under a military definition of reality. Given the accumulation of weapons of mass destruction, military decisions are by definition political decisions of the highest order. The military are involved in politics simply by their technical expertise.[17] We live in a time of military secrecy, lack of information, and Congress's virtual submission to the military. In short, neither the general public nor the Congress is able to effectively oversee the military. Decisions are made by the civilian secretary of defense or by the president and his civilian advisers, yes, but these decisions are based on information given by the military. Even Robert McNamara, considered by many to be the most resourceful, independent, and knowledgeable secretary of defense in recent times, never went against a unanimous decision of the Joint Chiefs of Staff.[18]

In short, the military has a substantial influence on the major decisions of our time. And when a military commitment is made (as in the case of Vietnam) their power increases because of the technical decisions that must be made. Mills is absolutely right in arguing that a military definition of reality, "a military metaphysic," pervades American society. Mills's problem is only his lack of precision in spelling out just how the military is equal to the political and economic elites. But given the secrecy that surrounds the military, a problem which leads us to the whole decision-making methodology in general, Mills was not too far off in his assertions about the military.

A Decision-Making vs. a Sociology-of-Leadership Approach

Of all the criticisms levelled against Mills, the most important one concerns his failure to take the decision-making process into account.[19] But a close look at this criticism tends to reveal more about Mills's critics than about *The Power Elite.* Daniel Bell, for instance, in his attempt to discredit Mills's thesis, refers to a "detailed analysis" by Richard Rovere of the decisions cited by Mills which "broadly refuted" the notion that the power elite was involved.[20] Upon close inspection the "detailed analysis" turns out to be a book review, a few paragraphs of which are devoted to a casual analysis of Mills's perspective. What is at work here is a not-so-curious double standard whereby little evidence is offered to support the pluralist framework while Mills is scored for not presenting definitive evidence.[21] For instance, William Kornhauser, himself a pluralist, writes the following concerning Mills's views and David Riesman's popular "veto-groups" concept: "In the absence of more disciplined historical and comparative analysis, we shall continue to lack a firm basis for evaluating such divergent diagnoses of political malaise as those given by Mills and Riesman."[22] Yet Kornhauser then comes out for Riesman's point of view. This in spite of the fact that only six pages of *The Lonely Crowd* are devoted to the "veto-groups," and no empirical evidence whatsoever is offered. The majority of social scientists who accept Riesman's notion of "veto-groups" or pluralistic equivalents are themselves adherents of a pluralistic interpretation of American politics. To envision them as objective analysts is pure intellectual naïveté.[23] Community power studies even if they do come up with evidence to support a pluralistic interpretation (and this is debatable)[24] do so only on a local level. What is forgotten, due to this emphasis upon local levels, is the inability of the social scientist to have access to important political decisions. Men who make the decisions that Mills attributes to the power elite, decisions about war and peace, slump and prosperity, make them privately. The social scientist is not invited. Furthermore, political leaders may lie outright to investigators, or distort either intentionally or possibly unintentionally what they have been involved in. For example, Robert Kennedy and Dean Acheson, both of whom were present during the Cuban missile crisis, have offered different versions of what "really happened."[25] The decision-making approach has serious shortcomings and should be used with caution.

This is what Mills was up against, and although his sociology-of-leadership approach by a positional or institutional analysis does not solve the problem, it does provide an alternative to the secrecy and deception that surrounds the making of important decisions. On the other hand, what have been offered as alternatives to Mills are scattered studies of local power structures, with an ideological bent (pluralism) inherent in the decision-making approach used. We are asked to believe that a power elite doesn't exist because Dahl, Polsby, *et al.*, did not find any evidence of a power elite in New Haven. Also, I cannot help questioning the accuracy of their analysis even on the modest level they set for themselves, when after they characterized New Haven as a smooth-running, efficient, progressive city, the "model city"—as it used to be called—"blew up" along with a number of other cities in the summer of 1967. The pluralists go wrong because their model emphasizes stability, with the government seen (according to Dahl) as a "relatively efficient system for maintaining peace in a restless and immoderate people."[26] Unless the people just got too restless all of a sudden, pluralism simply has not proven itself an accurate analytical device for understanding power. Nor will it, as long as it holds the implicit assumption that a balance theory of political power exists in American society when in practice certain segments (Mills argues both the lower and middle classes) are apparently prohibited from engaging in the political process.

In short, the pluralists have asked us to accept that a power elite does not exist in American society because, using decision-making approaches, they found no evidence to support its existence on a local level. Therefore, the pluralists (with one noted exception, Arnold Rose, who has studied the national scene and whose views I will now look at), have never really confronted Mills's theory of a power elite.

ARNOLD ROSE AND "THE POWER STRUCTURE"

The stated intention of Arnold Rose's work is an empirical attack on Mills and Floyd Hunter,[27] whose use of the reputational method led him to the same conclusions as Mills. Early in *The Power Structure* Rose writes:

The present book provides an empirically based critique of the Hunter-Mills hypothesis that the economic elite acts in a more-or-less unified fashion to control the political process of the United States. This hypothesis . . . is much older than the writings of Hunter and Mills, but never before has it received such careful formulation (as in Mills) or such an attempt at empirical foundation (as in Hunter and his followers). The hypothesis has received excellent scholarly criticism before this book was written, but by political scientists and political philosophers. Since Hunter and Mills are sociologists rather than political scientists, there might be special merit in a criticism by an empirically based sociologist who considers the same wide range of forces that Hunter and Mills consider. We shall oppose the Hunter-Mills economic-elite-dominance hypothesis with a multi-influence hypothesis. In doing so, we shall limit ourselves to a consideration of the political processes, and not concern ourselves with other areas of interest to Hunter and Mills.[28]

However, as one reads *The Power Structure*, it becomes evident that Rose does not realize this weighty ambition. He may have provided a scholarly refutation of Hunter's methodology (this is not a concern of the present work) but he has not added anything new to a refutation of Mills's thesis.

Rose's argument against Mills is marshalled in the case-study section of *The Power Structure*. The first empirical case study he offers is entitled "Political Structure and Political Influence in Texas." While it is an interesting and informative analysis of the political process in Texas and provides an astute analysis of the role Lyndon Johnson played, Rose's conclusions are applicable only to Texas. He ends the chapter on Texas politics with the following statement:

Texas has been thought of as a state in which economic influences over government have been especially strong, and yet we have seen that government and politics have a great deal of autonomous power. If our analysis has been largely correct, no interpretation of American politics can be made in terms of a limited number of structures and forces—such as a two party system, pressure groups representing largely economic forces, separation of executive from legislature, the expression of public opinion in voting—which operate throughout the United States. The reality is that all states are special cases, even if Texas is more special than most.[29]

Even assuming that Rose's interpretation is essentially correct, it has little or nothing to do with Mills's insistence that the power elite decides the really big issues at the national level.

Rose's second case study deals with "How Kennedy Won the Democratic Nomination" in 1960. Here we learn that Kennedy was not a white knight, that it costs money to get nominated for the presidency, and that the candidate has to be tough or politically skillful in gaining the nomination. These are hardly new or earthshaking revelations. In fact Domhoff argues in *Who Rules America?* that Kennedy was a Catholic member of the ruling class and by extension a member of the power elite. If anything, Rose's study of the Kennedy nomination leans more to supporting Mills than refuting it.

Rose's third empirical case study is "The Passage of Legislation: The Politics of Financing Medical Care for the Aging." Here we learn that it took Congress eight years to pass the 1965 Medicare bill and that the AMA was discredited in the process. Although it can be argued that the passage of a Medicare bill is a big issue, the importance or lack of importance of a power elite is never dealt with.

Rose's last chapter in this section is entitled "Some Problems of Politics: Money, Ethics, and Citizen Participation." Here he concludes that the candidate is not "bought but his campaign fund is."[30] Later on the reader is told that "A Gallup poll . . . of September 11, 1965 . . . showed that only 16 percent of a cross section of American adults ever served on a jury, only 19 percent ever write to a Congressman, and only 16 percent ever wrote a 'letter to the Editor.' "[31] If anything, Rose's comments tend to support rather than refute Mills's views on the existence of a power elite and the drift toward an apathetic mass society. In sum, Rose's view on how the political power structure functions does not offer, as he had hoped, a substantive refutation, by a sociologist, of C. Wright Mills's theory of a power elite. While Rose presents a description of how power may reinforce a pluralistic image of government at the local or middle levels of power, he is notably lacking when dealing with the governance of American society at the national level. He, like Dahl and Polsby, writes about conditions that are far removed from the level of power Mills is concerned with.

What we have then is no real substantive refutation of Mills's power elite thesis by his pluralistic critics. And as for his Marxist critics, their criticism is only slightly better than those of the pluralists.

MARXIST CRITICISMS

Although Mills's Marxist critics are generally pleased with his analysis, they still raise three important questions about *The Power Elite:* (1) Mills's view of the masses; (2) Mills's failure to deal with exploited minority groups; and (3) Mills's refusal to use the economic term *ruling class.*

The Masses

Most Marxist critics of Mills zero in on his views concerning America's masses. Robert Lynd writes that "Mills' failure to deal with the meanings for democracy of the impressive power trends he analyses is the colossal loose-end of *The Power Elite*"[32] while Herbert Aptheker accuses Mills of postulating a morally corrupt and generally powerless mass.[33] Both criticisms are unfair, because Mills never states that the United States is a mass society. Mills is interested in structural trends and sees America as merely heading in this direction. He is fairly explicit about this in *The Power Elite.*

The top of modern American society is increasingly unified, and often seems willfully co-ordinated: at the top there has emerged an elite of power. The middle levels are a drifting set of stalemated, balancing forces:

the middle does not link the bottom with the top. The bottom of this society is politically fragmented, and even as a passive fact, increasingly powerless: at the bottom there is emerging a mass society.[34]

The meaning for democracy is then simple: it is in great danger, given the structural trends which have produced a power elite. The masses are more apathetic than immoral, more lost than corrupt. What corruptness they manifest comes from the institutions that have shaped them. Aptheker, in particular, overlooks Mills's structural perspective and thereby fails to note that Mills is relating biography to social structure.

Mills's Failure to Consider Exploited Minority Groups

Aptheker is on firmer ground when he points out Mills's failure to mention "exploited minority groups,"[35] particularly blacks. Mills just never did deal with their plight. In light of what happened in the 1960's this is quite an omission. The only explanation, though by no means an excuse, is that Mills in spite of his non-Marxist power elite theory, was still influenced by Marx in his general habits of thought and saw racial and ethnic exploitation as merely incidental to a wider exploitation.[36]

Mills and the Concept "Ruling Class"

Mills's refusal to use the term *ruling class* seemed to bother his Marxist critics more than any other facet of his thesis. Paul Sweezy's remarks can be taken as representative:

No, the facts simply won't fit Mills' theory of three . . . elites coming together to form an overall power elite. What we have in the United States is a *ruling class* with its roots deeply sunk in the "apparatus of appropriation" which is the corporate system. To understand this ruling class—its metaphysics, its purposes, and its morals—we need to study, not certain "domains" of American life, however defined, but the whole system of monopoly capitalism.[37]

Mills is adamant about not using the concept "ruling class." Labelling his Marxist critics sarcastically as "True Radicals," he angrily writes at one point:

Since the war, neither business nor government can be understood as a separate realm of power. That is not enough for the True Radcials. They want to believe that the corporation and the state are identical, that they have become one big structure. Well, if not that, what do they mean? If they want me merely to evoke the good old party emotions that flood up in some people when they are told that the state is "a committee of the ruling class," I am sorry, I can't oblige: I don't believe it is quite that simple.[38]

On the whole, though, Mills is more in sympathy with his Marxist critics than one might infer from the above statement. His views towards Marxism and the existence of a power elite are best summed up in the following passage.

The study of elites does not rule out an acceptance of the kind of structural view one finds, for example, in Marx. In fact, one must pay attention to both. The historical structure of opportunity is more important, I hold, than 'the seizure of power' by elites of which some critics talk so much. The relation of institutional structure and elite formations is of course a two-sided play. Institutions, as I've repeatedly documented, select and form those who come to the top. In fact, sometimes the norms of selection and the shaping influences of institutional structures are more important to understanding human affairs and even the affairs of the powerful than the actual circles of men on top at any given time. I believe that is true just now, for example, in many corporations. But it's also true, given the shape of major institutions in the United States today, that those at the top are more than privileged persons: to a varying extent, in different historical situations, they are also powerful with all the means of power now at their disposal.[39]

Basically, then, neither Mills nor his Marxist critics prove their case beyond a doubt.

This, then, is Mills's position on the existence of a power elite in American society. Power is located in the institutional orders, which through the concept of role shape the character of those who come within its confines. Through co-optation,[40] the institutional orders select individuals, establish premiums and values, and generally mold the personality of the individual. Given the similarity of experience, of milieu, to use one of Mills's favorite terms, it would be of little consequence who is at the top in the institutional order. As Andrew Hacker points out:

To be sure, it is a lot easier to talk of people than positions, of individuals rather than institutions. For one thing, only the most technically-oriented reader can follow a discussion that omits personalities. Yet the really great social analysts—Marx, Weber, Veblen, Pareto—refused to be tempted in this direction. What is required, then, is an analysis of the great corporate institutions rather than the men who sit astride them.[41]

This is exactly what Mills does, and he establishes his place within the classical school of sociology. *The Power Elite* is a theory of stratification based upon Mills's general model of a social system. Mills's critics, pluralist or Marxist, have not substantiated their criticisms, and Mills's power elite thesis remains to this day one of the most important conceptions of power formulated by an American writer.

8

THE SOCIOLOGICAL IMAGINATION AND ITS USES

What is the sociological imagination that C. Wright Mills calls for? It is the model developed in *Character and Social Structure* with two additional ingredients: a more thorough grounding in history and a value-laden scheme of analysis. *The Sociological Imagination* is Mills's attempt to formulate a genuinely critical theory of society, an historical social-psychology that seeks to liberate the individual from the constraints of his social structure. Mills offers what the anthropologist Ernest Becker calls an "ideal-real" social science, an ideal science of man that serves both a moral-critical as well as a scientific-conceptual purpose.[1] Unlike Weber and the overwhelming majority of Mills's contemporaries, Mills stresses the importance of man's freedom. An ideal personality is emerging in American society—the "cheerful robot," the alienated individual who wants to become a cheerful and willing robot. The problem of this type of individual is to Mills the most important problem a social scientist could concern himself with. It is the major theme of the human condition, one around which contemporary social science has defaulted.[2] Mills, showing the influence of the pragmatists, stresses the importance of the use of reason to safeguard freedom. This now-open split with the objectivity of the Weberian tradition[3] does, however, raise a number of questions. Foremost is the relationship between political commitment, which Mills passionately advocates, and scholarly detachment, which social science is said to require. Indeed, a number of Mills's critics ask whether he is writing sociology after all, or whether his endeavors are more akin to journalism. In order to answer these questions we have to take a closer look at the modification of Mills's general model in *The Sociological Imagination.*

THE USES OF HISTORY

Social science must take into account the relation between biography and history and their intersection within particular social structures. This is the message of *The Sociological Imagination*. The sociologist is required to seek a comparative understanding of the social structures which have existed in the past and the present. The use of the sociological imagination brings with it the implication that smaller-scale milieux are to be selected and studied in terms of larger-scale historical and contemporary social structures. And most important of all the relation of institutions in all their varieties must be the main focus of the social scientist—this is what social structure is to Mills.

This emphasis upon social structure as the working unit of the sociologist leads to an analysis of power, for social structures are usually organized under political states, specifically nation-states. By choosing the nation-state, the investigator by definition concentrates upon major issues. At this level the means of power are organized, and power is tied intrinsically to history making.

Such problems as stratification, political power, economic power, economic policy, etc., cannot be adequately formulated without reference to a national framework. Sociologists in particular should bear this in mind, for historically the notion of social structure is most closely associated with the discipline of sociology.

To possess the sociological imagination is to do comparative work. The primary examples of such an endeavor are, of course, Weber's comparative historical studies. And Mills himself had tentative plans to embark on a comparative study of different social structures. Like Weber, who sees no one science explaining an inaccessible total reality, Mills holds that comparative emphasis directs the sociologist to cross over and transcend the boundaries of individual disciplines. Indeed, one could argue that Mills never really addresses himself to those who are usually called "sociologists," but through his constant interchanging of the terms *sociologist, intellectual,* and *social scientist* places himself squarely with those who advocate specialization not in terms of disciplinary structures but through the problems studied and the solutions offered. Mills's addition to this comparative sociology is his insistence that major institutions are not separate, that in terms of a particular social structure, various modes of integration and legitimation have to be taken into account.

This emphasis upon the comparative method is tied directly to an historical approach. The questions that must be asked lend themselves to such an endeavor; otherwise all investigation would be limited to mere description. Mills holds that historical studies by sociologists tended to be static or

at best very short term studies of limited milieux. The chance to understand how smaller milieux are related to larger causes requires the sociologist to deal with historical materials. Although the institutional formations and the resultant model or ideal type personalities produced are
unique for each social structure, this does not preclude the comparison of
social structures. The sociologist must grasp the particular mechanisms,
Mannheim's *principia media,* Mills's "mode of integration." Or, as Mills
put it, "There is . . . no 'law' stated by any social scientist that is trans-
historical that must not be understood as having to do with the specific
structure of some period."[4]

The biographies of men and women—the types of individuals who come
to prevail in a specific period—cannot be understood without reference to
an historical perspective. Man, as noted previously, cannot in the Millsian
system be understood simply as a biological creature who reacts to certain
stimuli in his environment. For as Mills states, "Whatever else he may be,
man is a social and an historical actor who must be understood if at all, in
close and intricate interplay with social and historical structures."[5]

Along with this emphasis upon the historical grounding of social structures, Mills also reiterates the psychological base or more explicitly the
social psychology of his model. Indeed, in a footnote on page 161 of *The
Sociological Imagination,* he refers the reader to *Character and Social
Structure* for a more detailed discussion of the implications of social
psychology for the sociological imagination. In both works the concern is
not with academic psychology, but with a kind of psychoanalytical approach to institutional behavior. Mills asks for an expansion of the type of
analysis done by psychoanalysts on the nature of the family's impact upon
personality, one which would do the same for all institutions.

The psychological concerns of this "new" social science look to biography, social roles, institutions, and their interrelationship. In a passage
that could have come straight out of *Character and Social Structure,* Mills
writes:

The view of man as a social creature enables us to go much deeper than
merely the external biography as a sequence of social roles. Such a view
requires us to understand the most internal and "psychological" feature of
man: in particular, his self-image and his conscience and indeed the very
growth of his mind. It may well be that the most radical discovery within
recent psychology and social science is the discovery of how so many of
the most intimate features of the person are socially patterned and even
implanted within the broad limits of the glandular and nervous apparatus;
the emotions of fear and hatred and love and rage in all their varieties must
be understood in close and continual reference to the social biography and
the social context in which they are experienced and expressed. Within

the broad limits of the psychology of the sense organs, our very perception of the physical world, the colors we discriminate, the smells we become aware of, the noises we hear, are socially patterned and socially circumscribed. The motivations of men and even the varying extents to which various types of men are typically aware of them are to be understood in terms of the vocabularies of motive that prevail in a society and of social changes and confusions among such vocabularies.[6]

Thus, Mills's expanded general model of a social structure enables him to not only locate the individual within his historical milieu, but also to deal with his psychological reactions to it. Where does this use of a model grounded in history, the sociological imagination, lead to? According to Mills, the climax of the social scientist's concern with history is "the idea he comes to hold of the epoch in which he lives. The climax of his concern with biography is the idea he comes to hold of man's basic nature and of the limits it may set to the transformation of man by the course of history."[7]

MILLS'S IDEAL-REAL SOCIOLOGY

Mills's ideal-real sociology represents his attempts to formulate a critical sociology; to do this, Mills attacked the prevailing sociology of the 1950's, a sociology which was anything but critical.

Mills's original efforts in this direction date back to his famous "The Professional Ideology of the Social Pathologists" (1943); there, working in the area of the sociology of knowledge, he questioned the objectivity of the social pathologists of that time. Mills's concern in the late 1940's was with labor, and it wasn't until the early 1950's that he again picked up the theme of values in social science. In two articles, "Two Styles of Social Science Research" and "IBM Plus Reality Plus Humanism = Sociology," written in 1953 and 1954 respectively,[8] the antecedents of *The Sociological Imagination* are clear.

In "Two Styles of Social Science Research," Mills postulates the existence of two modes of inquiry in contemporary social science: the macroscopic and the molecular. These in turn bring about two senses of craftsmanship. The macroscopic tradition claims Weber, Marx, Michels, Simmel, and Mannheim, to name just a few classical thinkers. Social structures, general types of historical phenomena, interconnecting institutional orders, and a general relating to the prevailing types produced in any given society are the data handled by the macroscopic sociologists. The molecular tradition is characterized by small-scale problems and statistical models of verification. Mills is extremely sarcastic in his descriptions of the microscopic branch of sociology, reducing it to an emphasis upon technique and little else. There are at least three substantive differences of a logical sort between the macroscopic and molecular style of research, with the molecular mode opting for more objectivity, cumulative development, and statistical quantification. Objectivity implies that another researcher can repeat the work of his predecessors and come to the same result provided there were no procedural errors. Out of this replication comes accumulation. The macroscopic tradition, which is more subjective, is characterized by a taking up where others left off; it leads to a continuity of subject matter, ideas, and approach rather than a statistical accumulation of data.

Mills envisions a joining of the two styles of work. The sociologist who could combine both traditions would have the best of two worlds—a general conceptual scheme and an index of general variables to substantiate the particular conceptual scheme. All the sociologist has to do is break down the macroscopic conceptions and build up the molecular terms. Mills closes the article with a call for the macroscopic researchers to use their imaginations more technically and for the technicians to go about their work with more imaginative concern for macroscopic meaning as well as technical ingenuity.

One year later, in 1954, Mills published "IBM Plus Reality Plus Humanism = Sociology," in which he modified somewhat his thoughts on the macroscopic and molecular styles of sociological endeavor. At this time Mills divided American sociology into three main camps, a division he would later incorporate into *The Sociological Imagination.* The three camps are the scientists, a subspecies of the higher statistician; the grand theorists; and the third camp, which Mills does not name but deems the only one worthy of being called sociologist. This latter group has three major tasks: (1) to ask what the meaning of certain phenomena is in relation to the society as a whole; (2) to ask what the meaning is for the types of men and women that prevail in the society; and (3) to ask how the main drift is carrying us.[9]

It is obvious that when Mills writes of the "sociological enterprise" and of those who are worthy of the name sociologist, he is speaking of those social scientists who use something like his own general model. It would become the "sociological imagination" when he emphasizes the importance of history. Even more so than in these two articles, Mills, in *The Sociological Imagination,* is extremely biting in his description of the opposing schools of sociology. In this respect he is quite similar to Veblen, who uses the same method of attack and to whom Mills is so often compared. The three divisions Mills now labels "The Abstracted Empiricists," "The Grand Theorists," and either the "Philosophers of History" or the possessors of the "sociological imagination."

The Grand Theorists and The Abstracted Empiricists are attacked because of their failure to use the "sociological imagination." The two leading figures of these schools, Talcott Parsons and Paul Lazarsfeld, respectively, are singled out for assault. Mills's chapter on Parsons and Grand Theory is satire at its best, but, as Dennis Wrong points out, may be a bit too harsh.

He [Mills] makes much of the opaqueness of Parsons' terminology and effectively ridicules it by quoting huge gobs and then "translating" them into a few brief and lucid sentences. I have no desire to defend Parsons' prose, which has to be read to be believed, but it does have more content than Mills' jibes suggest.[10]

A critique or analysis of Parsons's work is well beyond the scope of this work; however, Mills's criticisms can be summarized here. He believes that there is no single grand theory, no universal scheme in terms of which we can understand the unity of social structure. There just is not one answer to the problem of social order. The general problem of history should not—indeed, cannot—be separated from the general problem of the theory of social structure. Parsons assumes that there is one answer to the question of what holds a social structure together. Mills, on the other hand, feels that there are a number of answers, because social structures differ in terms of unity. In Mills's scheme, social structures are to be analyzed according to their different modes of integration. His answer is to put forth "a set of 'working models' which are used to make us more aware, as we examine specific societies at specific times, of the links by which they are 'tied together.'"[11] These "modes of integration" are offered as "working models" of social change. The social scientist analyzes how the various institutional orders have changed and how this change is related to the other institutional orders. In short, Mills uses his own general model of a social system, or "the sociological imagination" as an alternative to Grand Theory or Parsonian sociology.

Mills's attack on the empirical school is also both an exercise in satirical exposition and a critique based upon his perspective of a general model of a social system. Mills argues that the "Abstracted Empiricists" are more concerned with scientific methods than with sociology itself. They embrace one philosophy of science and equate it with the scientific method. The result is a methodological inhibition, since methodological techniques determine the problem, not the other way around.

An example of what the "Abstracted Empiricists" have accomplished is the celebrated study of Erie County, Ohio, in 1940, reported in *The Peoples Choice*. According to Mills, all the reader learns from this work is that "rich, rural and Protestant persons tend to vote Republican; people of opposite type incline toward the Democrats; and so on. But we learn little about the dynamics of American politics."[12]

Mills is even more biting when he discusses the young men who choose Abstracted Empiricism as a career.

As often as not they have not had adequate college work; at least there are reasons to suspect—although I do not know—that there is a selection of not quite the brightest for such research insitutions.

I have seldom seen one of these young men, once he is well caught up, in a condition of genuine intellectual puzzlement. And I have never seen any passionate curiosity. . .that compels the mind to travel and by any means to re-make itself if necessary in order to find out. These young men are less restless than methodical; less imaginative than patient; above all they are dogmatic in all the historical meanings of the term. Some of this is, of course, merely part of the sorry intellectual condition of so many students now in American Colleges and Universities but it is more evident among the research technicians of abstracted empiricism.[13]

As with Parsons, Mills's major criticism of this school revolves around the use of a working model. The Abstracted Empiricists have none. Their "theory" subsequently consists only of the variables they use and in practice is restricted to statistically determined facts and relationships.

Mills contends that if these two schools were the only two in American sociology, little if anything would become known about man and his relationship to society. There is, of course, a third alternative, a return to the notion of sociology as philosophy of history—a tradition that claims Weber, Marx, Mannheim, Comte, and Spencer. Implicit in this view of sociology and stressed in *Character and Social Structure, Images of Man,* and in *The Sociological Imagination* is the creation of working models. Therein lie the weaknesses of Grand Theory and Abstracted Empiricism. Classical sociologists proceed from a working model. Not only is this the theme of the three works mentioned above, but is also implicit in Mills's last work, *The Marxists* (1962), in which Mills uses his working model to criticize both Marxist and liberal models of history.

After his attack on the leading schools of sociology Mills had to offer something in their place. This is the meaning of *The Sociological Imagination.* Mills could never discard the epistemological basis of pragmatism, the notion that the mind is not a passive spectator in the knowing process—that knowledge is intrinsically related to activity. His position, which forms a large part of *The Sociological Imagination,* differs from that of the pragmatists only in that Mills does not see reason as naturally leading to freedom. The individual, in order to be free, has to be aware of the structural constraints which envelop his existence. His path to freedom lies in his knowing what these constraints are and intervening to do something about them. The possessor of the sociological imagination has the ability to transcend his own milieu and take a step toward freedom. Mills attaches a metaphysical basis to reason and freedom; they become value judgments to him. He presents to us in *The Sociological Imagination* a means through which we can develop an historical critique of contemporary social structures. We are shown how and why man is not free. A path which leads to freedom in each epoch or historical period is to be set before us. There is nothing in man's basic nature that renders him incapable of attaining freedom; it is only his ignorance of how he is constrained that enslaves him to his social structure. If only individuals could be made aware; if only enough men could be reached, perhaps then radical change would come about, says Mills. Near the end of his career Mills was still professing a populist creed, but one that was honed by insights fashioned out of twenty years of being a professional sociologist. With *The Sociological Imagination,* Mills makes a major break with academic sociology. Writing of what could be and not what is, Mills brings into American sociology the critical faculty it lacks. *The Sociological Imagination* is an angry book; the emperor had been naked for a long time and the news was shouted in a loud voice. However, along with this anger there crops up in Mills's later works the old problem of the reconciliation of activism and scholarship. Given his definition of reality as one in which the power elite makes history, it is incumbent upon Mills to clarify how the reality can be changed. Attempting to solve this problem, Mills again reaches back to his pragmatic roots. The psychological or personality part of Mills's model follows Dewey's rejection of an unchanging "human nature" and of a psychology of "instincts" as explanations of the continuity of social institutions. This continuity is explained in terms of socially acquired "customs" and "habits," and because "habit means will"[14] the repeated daily activities of individuals are voluntary acts.[15] The implication here is that institutions and by extension society can be changed through human activity, that collective actions can have social consequences, and therefore radical change is possible. Because Dewey's concept of action is individual and not political, it is rejected by Mills. A political strategy must be based on a definition of reality which can be changed by collective activity, by political activity which appeals to others. For Dewey, the others form the "Public," a community of self-directed individuals.[16] The intellectual could be linked to the public via communication. For Dewey this occurs through education; social reform comes out of educational reform. Mills, however, chooses a more direct channel of access to the public, that of the mass media. The 1950's had witnessed the impact of paperback publishing, and the implications were startling to Mills. The intellectual could reach a mass audience, millions of readers, through inexpensive paperback books.

Mills's assumptions for radical change are rooted in his view of man as potentially free. The question he constantly asks—Do men make history?—is answered affirmatively for America in the middle of the twentieth century. In societies where the means of power are rudimentary and decentralized, history is *fate;* but where the means of power are enormous and centralized, a few men strategically placed do make history. On this Mills is quite clear: men are free to make history, though some are freer than others. Freedom requires access to the means of decision by which history can be made. The intellectuals have defaulted by withdrawing from politics, and in actuality simply serve those who are in power. The intellectuals must repossess the cultural apparatus for their own purposes. They should write and speak in the media on their own terms or not at all.[17] Although Mills obviously believes that the possessor of the sociological imagination is freer than most, this position is not an elitist one. The average citizens, those who make up the "public," also possess a certain amount of freedom. In a 1950 article, "Mass Media and Public Opinion," Mills writes that the presidential election of Harry S. Truman shows that:

No view of American public life can be realistic that assumes public opinion to be wholly controlled and entirely manipulated by the mass media. There are forces at work among the public that are independent of the media of communication, that can and do at times go directly against the opinions promulgated by them.[18]

The average individual therefore carries with him a real potential for freedom, and it is up to the intellectuals to make him realize this potential. Intellectuals are thus in a unique position to make a new beginning, and this entails that they stop whining about alienation and instead advocate radical critiques and programs for the future. In short, the intellectual must redefine reality. For if he doesn't, asks Mills, who will?

This is just what Mills tries to do in *The Causes of World War III* (1958) and *Listen, Yankee* (1960)—he wants to take up the role of the moral conscience of the society, to force the power elite to be responsible to the "public." Unfortunately, these works are Mills's poorest. There is evidence, however, that Mills was aware that his "pamphlets" as he called them (particularly *Listen, Yankee*) lacked something. His discussions with Harvey Swados, his debating with himself over denouncing *Listen, Yankee,* along with his unpublished works all point to the possibility that Mills was becoming extremely cautious about defining strategies for change, that he was struggling with the notion that he was much better at analyzing than at acting. Witness in particular the following unpublished passage from *Tovarich:*

The most important single non-routine task in the world today is to try and define the realities of what may be going on, in terms of the ideals of western civilization. Last year, a friend of mine in Warsaw reported to me what Marx said about philosophers not just interpreting the world but changing it. Then he added: "We must just now, reverse that: the point is to interpret it." I understand why my Polish friend should say that, just then, but I think its time beyond those reasons. At any rate, even if I didn't like it, it's true for me.[19]

Although Mills's untimely death makes the above mere speculation, we can see that *Images of Man* (1960) and *The Marxists* (1962) definitely stress analysis and not action.

"IMAGES OF MAN" AND "THE MARXISTS"

In *Images of Man*, Mills tells us why he chooses the selections he does and what he believes to be *the* characteristic in the thought of the classical sociologists. It is, of course, their use of "models." The classical sociologists continue to exert influence upon contemporary social scientists because they formulated and used models as the basis of their analysis.

In *The Marxists* Mills carries this notion of a model further, using it to criticize liberalism and Marxism. Here Mills reiterates much of what he had said in previous articles, particularly a 1952 essay entitled "Liberal Values in the Modern World,"[20] where he reduces both socialism and liberalism to mere rhetoric, indicting them for becoming ideologies of one particular status quo or another. Liberalism in America is divorced from political reality. It no longer clarifies or explains what is occurring in twentieth-century America. Liberalism holds, as an underlying assumption, the notion that freedom and security flourish in the world of small entrepreneurs, whereas the past one hundred years had seen a shift in the scale of property units. Liberty once involved the control of one's own property, but now the centralization of property control produces anxiety instead. The individual is dependent upon large property holdings and can no longer provide for his own future. The question for liberals, then, revolves around a confrontation of old individualistic ideas with new social and psychological factors. Individual freedom anchored to the security of small property holdings and small communities is a thing of the past. The problem of liberals is a problem of rearticulation, of trying to remain a moral force in a world where they are strangers.

Mills, while positing the same theme in *The Marxists*, goes a bit further and stresses the inability of the liberal to see the whole structure of society. Liberalism does not look at society as a whole; it has no grasp of history. It is merely the ideology of the entrepreneurial middle class. In short, liberalism lacks a working model of the social system in which it is ensconced. Mills uses the same argument he used previously to criticize Grand Theory and Abstracted Empiricism. Marxism, on the other hand, does have an underlying working model, but according to Mills, it is an inadequate one. Mills, however, is quick to point out that Marx, while somewhat mistaken in his overall view, still offers a model that presents a master scheme for viewing: "(1) the structure of society; (2) the mechanics of the history of that society; and (3) the roles of individuals in all their psychological nuances."[21] As we saw in chapter one, Mills holds that what is important is not the truth or falsity of the theories based upon the model, but the model itself. Marx's model could be used for the construction of many theories as well as correcting those made with its aid.[22]

Yet, though Mills considers Marx *the* political thinker of the twentieth century, that thinker whom social scientists had to be familiar with to be even considered social scientists, this does not preclude his offering a trenchant criticism of Marx. According to Mills, the Marxist model assumes a society in which the typical units are small in scale and autonomous, as is in a free market economy. Capitalism is too advanced for such a model.

Since Marx's day, the social structures of capitalism have changed to such an extent as to require a new statement of the causal weight of economic institutions, and of their causal relations with other institutions. . .

Many twentieth-century economic developments must themselves be explained by changes in political and military forces. I do not mean to replace "economic determinism," by "political determinism" or "military determinism," but only to suggest that the causal weight of each of these types is not subject to any historically universal rule. It must be historically determined in the case of any given society.[23]

Marx, like the Grand Theorists, postulates a universal model. Given Mills's own working-model approach, Marx's model constitutes an inadequate construction. Mills, though believing one had to come to grips with Marxism, indeed, had to use it, never fully accepts Marxism as a total world view. Given his own background in pragmatism and its emphasis upon the freedom of the individual, Mills could never accept what he considered to be the determinism of Marx. Mills states implicitly in *The Marxists* that he believes Marx to be a determinist. He could not be clearer on this than in the following paragraphs:

Marx is a determinist for the following reasons:
(a) The question of the historical agency is clearly bound up with the problem of historical inevitability and with the ideal of socialism. . . . .

(b) Marx's refusal to preach ideals and his reluctance to discuss the society of the future makes no sense otherwise. . . .

(c) He did not try to persuade men of any new moral goals, because he believed that the proletariat would inevitably come to them. "In the last analysis," social existence determines consciousness. Historical developments will implant these goals into the consciousness of men, and men will act upon them. The individual has little choice. If his consciousness is not altogether determined, his choice is severely limited and pressed upon him by virtue of his class position and all the influences and limitations to which this leads. . . .

(d) Historically, the idea of progress has been fully incorporated into the very ethos of Marxism. Marx re-seats this idea—in the development of the proletariat. . . .[24]

Marx stated clearly the doctrine of economic determinism. It is reflected in his choice of vocabulary; it is assumed by, and fits into, his work as a whole—in particular his theory of power, his conception of the state, his rather simple notions of class and his use of these notions (including the proletariat as the agency of history-making). We may of course assume with Engels that he allows a degree of free-play among the several factors that interact, and also that he provides a flexible time-schedule in which economic causes do their work. But in the end—and usually the end is not very far off—economic causes are "the basic, the ultimate, the general, the innovative causes of historical change."[25]

To the pragmatically trained Mills, such a determinism is anathema. Only his own working model, his synthesis of pragmatism and German sociology, could take the problem of freedom and choice into consideration. Mills's final conclusion concerning Marxism is that the general trend of history has rendered much of Marxist theory inadequate. The Marxist model is something that the social scientist must contend with; it is part of his homework; but as an adequate conceptual scheme it leaves much to be desired. In short, Mills tries to go beyond Marxism by opting for his own working model over that of Marx.

Although *The Marxists* is Mills's last published book, at the time of his death he was working on *Comparative Sociology* (the proposed title), which was to be a six or more volume study of present-day social structures. Here Mills, by using the concept of epoch, which he touches upon in *The Sociological Imagination* and spells out in more detail in a 1959 article entitled "Culture and Politics,"[26] attempts to place contemporary societies in their historical settings. Societies are to be looked at in terms of ancient, medieval, industrial, and post-industrial epochs. In the following passage from *Comparative Sociology* we can see how Mills was going to apply the "sociological imagination":

External events and historical trends are not enough. To make our point that we are indeed being moved into a new epoch of human history requires, first, that we show a shift or a change in the psychological bearings of the individual's biography and character; and second, intellectually, moreover, we must show that the very categories of explanation which served to orient men in past epochs no longer are satisfactory in the present epoch. It is this fact that is most central in defining an epoch. For the explanation on which men lean sets up for them what they expect and what they hope for. And it is by means of the "hoped for" that we can most readily enter into the meaning of an epoch for human and psychological values.[27]

Mills is interested in locating whole structures of societies within epochs. *The Sociological Imagination* grounded his working model in history; it could now be used for a monumental study of modern social structures. Whether or not he could have brought off such an enormous endeavor can only be the basis of speculation. Death claimed C. Wright Mills at the moment he was about to begin.

9

PAYING HOMAGE TO THE FATHER:
C. WRIGHT MILLS AND RADICAL SOCIOLOGY

C. Wright Mills is almost universally acknowledged to be the father of what has come to be known as "radical sociology."[1] His attacks on objectivity and value-free social science[2] as well as his political writings[3] signalled the beginnings of this new school in sociology. However, as is often the case with "founding fathers," homage is being paid for other than the most important reasons. What seems to be occurring is that Mills is being looked upon more as a romantic hero than as a social theorist. Given the legendary qualities Mills possessed, along with the lack of a heroic tradition among academics, this is quite easily done. Mills's feuds with other sociologists; the rumors about his sex life; the anecdotes about him as a graduate student at Wisconsin; his riding to his classes at Columbia on a BMW motorcycle; his early death, all have made him something of a Hemingway character, an existential man who was always saying "No," in thunder.

Unfortunately, however, such a portrait fails to consider that Mills's cries were based on his being first and foremost a sociologist, and a very good one—that, as I have tried to show throughout this work, there is in Mills's total works a comprehensive model of man and society and their relationship in history. That Mills worked from a model is even more significant given the fact that those radical sociologists who acclaim Mills have failed to produce a substantive social theory from which their critiques of society can be mounted. The only alternative to what is perceived as conservative structural-functionalism are diverse forms of Marxism which as yet have not been synthesized into any cohesive model which posits an adequate notion of social structure without sacrificing the active, volitional side of man.[4]

FUNCTIONALISM, CONFLICT, AND VARIETIES OF MARXISM

Steven Deutsch has written that "radical sociology may well lead to calls for action, but first it will master a perspective which is structural and which calls for basic change, not minor alterations in social structures. . . ."[5] To this I would add that if such a perspective is to be a liberating one it must hold a view of man as free or at least potentially free. In short, I would paraphrase George Gurwitsch's famous definition of sociology[6] as follows: radical sociology is the study of human freedom and of all the structural obstacles which this freedom encounters and overcomes in part. My position is that the models of analysis around which radical sociologists have rallied have not solved the basic dilemma of human volition and structural constraint, and that C. Wright Mills has. I am not interested in Parsonian functionalism as having any radical potential, believing that functionalism has been a dead horse for many years and was finally given a decent burial by Alvin Gouldner.[7] The same can be said of the non-Marxist conflict perspective, which for a time was considered quite radical[8] but no longer holds any appeal for radicals. Interestingly enough, two of the more famous advocates of this type of conflict perspective, John Rex and Ralf Dahrendorf, have in their recent works[9] come to rely so heavily on the deterministic aspects of the concept of role that they have moved away from any view of conflict as a liberating paradigm, seeing man simply as a plastic player of roles. In *Race, Community and Conflict* (1967), a work by John Rex and Robert Moore, the individual is envisioned as becoming whatever the social system requires of him. Man is infinitely maleable and manipulable, and the social structure and the concept of role with its assumptions of social-psychological determinism does the defining.[10] As for Dahrendorf, witness the following from his essay, "Homo Sociologicus" (1968):

> To become a part of society and a subject of sociological analysis, man must be socialized, chained to the fact of society and made its creature. By observation, imitation, indoctrination, and conscious learning, he must grow into the forms that society holds in readiness for him as an incumbent of positions. . . .
> For society and sociology, socialization invariably means depersonalization, the yielding up of man's absolute individuality and liberty to the constraint and generality of social rules.[11]

What seems to be on the surface a more promising approach, at least in terms of possible support from radical sociologists, is Erving Goffman's dramaturgical model. However, a close reading of Goffman's theory shows an almost complete lack of a coherent notion of social structure, and he fails to analyze the nature of power and its ramifications. What we have, then, is a very limited view of how men effect change. Indeed, Goffman has always been much more concerned with how men adapt to social conditions than to how they might be liberated from them.[12] Perhaps Alvin Gouldner has best summarized Goffman's precarious relationship with the New Left.

Goffman's avoidance or rejection of conventionalized hierarchicalizations has . . . important ambiguities to it. On the one side, it has an implication of being *against* the existent hierarchies and hence against those advantaged by it; it is, to this extent, infused with a rebel vision critical of modern society. On the other side, however, Goffman's rejection of hierarchy often expresses itself as an *avoidance* of social stratification and of the importance of power differences, even for concerns that are central to him; thus it entails an accommodation to existent power arrangements. Given this ambiguity, response to Goffman's theories is often made selectively, the viewer focusing on the ambiguity congenial to him, and thus some among the rebellious young may see it as having a "radical potential."[13]

Basically, then, when we speak of radical sociology today, we speak of Marxist sociology—a sociology with two major branches, phenomenological and scientific.[14] Advocates of the former adhere to the writings of the young Marx, while the latter embrace the mature Marx's materialistic and deterministic views. Although there have been attempts at synthesizing the two views,[15] given the disparity of presuppositions among these two schools, it seems highly unlikely that any real reconciliation will take place in the near future. A case in point is an ideological debate that recently took place in the pages of *The Insurgent Sociologist* (a Marxist journal which is the closest thing to an official organ of radical sociology) between Richard Pozzuto and Al Szymanski, spokesman for phenomenological and scientific Marxism respectively. In order to better locate their debate in terms of Mills's model, I will deal only with those points which pertain to their view of volition, social structure, and their concomitant ramifications for liberation.

Liberation is almost impossible in the phenomenological Marxist perspective because, as Szymanski perceptively points out, phenomenologists

hold the idealist doctrine that the social world is essentially a product of the ideas men hold of it, i.e., that men's conceptions or social definitions of social relations essentially determine the nature of social relations, and the related subjectivist notions that men can change the social world by merely understanding the nature of social relations is enough to get men to will to change them are inherently false, conservative and misleading principles for movements of the oppressed to operate on. If social relations are a product of men's mind, then the course to follow if a movement wants to change the world is to change men's heads.[16]

The logical result of the phenomenological view is that consciousness is the determinant of social reality, and individuals can thereby change their condition by an act of will. One step further brings us to the proposition that it is not society that oppresses people but their own attitudes. This is, of course, a perfect example of the "blaming the victim"[17] ideology so common in American society. Yet what does Szymanski offer as an alternative to the essentially social-structureless view he attacks. He gives us a materialistic, deterministic, and "scientific" sociology. Social change, to him, is an inevitable outcome of deterministic laws. "Social relations have a logic of their own which ... determine behavior."[18] Szymanski's radical Marxist sociology is, therefore, devoid of free choice. "All social phenomena are determined by social, biological or environmental forces independent of men's will and normally of their consciousness as well."[19] In short, Szymanski asks us to accept extreme positivism, which treats as unproblematic the notion that social phenomena possess the same characteristics as natural phenomena. But as David Walsh has recently argued,

positivism explains social order as being "out there" in an external social world produced by relationships between factors external to the members of that world. ... But this not only leads to an illegitimate reification of society but more specifically avoids crucial issues about how a shared social world is possible at all.[20]

Szymanski's positivism would have us ignore Marx's notion of a dialectic relationship between man and society. For as Richard Pozzuto states:

Szymanski's notion of Marx as a materialist and a determinist is a step backward from the actual achievements of Marx. If we were to follow the framework of Szymanski's argument that Marx is a determinist we would find no political task for human actors. If as Szymanski states human behavior is "completely determined," then it is not important to study people nor is it what they actually do since their actions are not directed by themselves but rather by forces external to them. We, as actors, can have no effect on the world if people are mere pawns. If forces external to us direct our every activity, it is those forces that contain the destiny of man, not man himself.[21]

Basically, then, Pozzuto is quite right when he points up Szymanski's failure to confront Husserl's basic premise in *The Crisis of European Sciences*—that the crisis of social science is not one of reconstructed logic, but a crisis about knowing, whether in the natural or the social sciences.

What we are left with then is a seemingly irreconcilable dilemma between the phenomenological and scientific schools of Marxism. The former assumes that man is free, but it lacks a coherent view of social structure; the latter postulates a deterministic social structure with individuals seen in behavioristic terms. In a nutshell, then, the fundamental dilemma of radical Marxist sociology is that when it opts for an active view of man it lacks a conception of social structure, and when it posits a notion of social structure, volition is sacrificed. What, then, is the answer? Do we somehow try to reconcile these two views by stressing the continuities in the work of the young and the mature Marx, as the phenomenologists have done?[22] Or do we accept the notion that there is a quantum leap between the humanism of the 1844 manuscripts and the political economies of *Capital*— that for all intents and purposes there are "two Marxisms."[23] My answer leans toward the latter. I believe these two schools of Marxism are irreconcilable; but more important, even if they are not, Marx's model of society has been overturned by historical events. I agree here with C. Wright Mills, who states:

The model as Marx left it is inadequate. One can use it only with great intellectual clumsiness and wasted sophistication, and often only with doubletalk.[24]

What is needed is not a synthesis of divergent views of Marxism but a going beyond Marx. Marx's work should only be a beginning point, not a finished view of the world. What is needed is a more comprehensive model, an historical social-psychological one that analyzes the interplay between personality formation and social structures. Marxism, whatever its variety, assumes a simplistic, rationalistic psychological theory within a system shaped by the primacy of economic interests. What is needed is a model that shows that economic means are only one means of power and may very well be determined by political and military aims and interests in different historical epochs—a model that can account satisfactorily for the origin of mind while at the same time showing how meanings are built into the human organism. C. Wright Mills constructed such a model. Whether or not this model is still in the Marxist tradition is inconsequential given that it is a radical structural model. Call it what you will, "neo-Marxist," "plain-Marxist," or "non-Marxist"—even to debate such a question is counterproductive. What is important is Mills's shift away from pure economic determinism along with the addition of a nonpassive theory of personality formation. By coming to radicalism from a different perspective than that of the traditional Marxists—American pragmatism and Weberian sociology—Mills was able to construct a view of man, perhaps not straining against himself, as the anthropologist Ernest Becker calls for,[25] but one where man struggles against an oppressive social structure. Mills postulates an historical model of a social system to explain why human conduct assumes the form it does in each epoch. In short, he offers a sociological paradigm to analyze the manner in which psychological regularities are affected and shaped by historical social structures.

Mills offers us a model that is liberating, one that possesses an adequate conception of social structure and yet does not sacrifice the volitional, active nature of man. Mills points out a path toward freedom. Because of his early training in pragmatism, Mills never gives up the notion of the autonomous individual who could use his reason to gain and secure his freedom. Like Marx, Mills believes man is alienated, given the society he lives in; but where Marx saw alienation as a result of the irrationality of production, Mills sees it coming from man's perception of and adaptation to a society in blind drift. In order to be free, the individual has to make the connection between "private troubles" and "public issues." He has to be aware that structural problems are the key to his malaise. Only by seeing the interconnection of biography and history could man begin to gauge the limits of his potential. This is the fundamental message of *The Sociological Imagination* and is explicit in Mills's working model approach. The social scientist must look at the structure of society as a whole and at the ways in which its institutions shape the character of individuals. But more than this, Mills argues, the social scientist must "study the structural limits of human decision in an attempt to find points of effective intervention, in order to know what can and what must be structurally changed if the role of explicit decision in history-making is to be enlarged."[26] He should study historical structures in order to find ways which can insure the freedom of individuals. Beyond this locating of where the structure could best be changed lay the political problem of decision making and the intellectual problem of discerning the structural limits of man's basic nature.

Mills's working model approach enables the social scientist to transcend the realm of private troubles, to see that structural problems are at the root of man's alienation. Reason could lead to freedom when and if the individual became aware that "rationally organized arrangements . . . often . . . are a means of tyranny and manipulation."[27] It is for the social scientist to point out how man can be free in his society, to try to insure this freedom by intervening to make the structure of society less repressive.

Mills offers a picture of man as free but constrained by power relations. In this view, some men are freer than others and are thereby responsible for their acts. History is made behind most men's backs, not behind all men's backs. There are various degrees of freedom. Through the use of the model, power and those in positions of power, not necessarily economic elites, can be located. Who they are, why they are powerful is a problem for investigation by the sociologist. What we have in Mills's model is not an "invidious doctrine" of free-will which can be used to justify punishment and repression when men are perceived as responsible for their actions,[28] as some scientific Marxists might argue, but a doctrine of moral responsibility in the face of societal constraint. Man is free, but some men are freer than others.

C. Wright Mills provided a working model of a social system which enables its users to analyze just how much the individual is constrained by his social structure. In doing so Mills left a cohesive, systematic, historical sociology—a model that can provide the structural perspective radical sociology currently lacks. At present, radical sociologists who see themselves working in the tradition of C. Wright Mills, in spite of their criticisms of "establishment" sociology,[29] have produced little, if any, important criticism of American society, and no substantive social theory for doing so. Instead of paying homage to Mills for his actions, we should now honor him for his intellect as well. Mills left us a sociological map in the form of a general model of a social system, a model that can help to resolve the contradictions in Marxism. It is now up to those who consider themselves as working in the tradition of C. Wright Mills to come to grips with Mills's sociological legacy. In short, what is necessary is an acceptance of C. Wright Mills as a systematic social theorist. In this way, we can begin to pay homage to the father of radical sociology, to the man who may very well be "the greatest sociologist the United States has ever produced."[30]

ABBREVIATIONS USED IN THE NOTES

CSS   Hans Gerth and C. Wright Mills. *Character and Social Structure.*
New York: Harcourt, Brace and World, 1953.

IM   C. Wright Mills, ed. *Images of Man.* New York: George
Braziller, Inc., 1970.

LY   C. Wright Mills. *Listen, Yankee: The Revolution in Cuba.* New
York: Ballantine Books, 1960.

NMP   C. Wright Mills. *The New Men of Power.* New York: Harcourt,
Brace and World, 1948.

PE   C. Wright Mills. *The Power Elite.* New York: Oxford University
Press, 1956.

PPP   C. Wright Mills. *Power, Politics and People: The Collected
Essays of C. Wright Mills,* ed. Irving Louis Horowitz. New York:
Oxford University Press, 1964.

SI   C. Wright Mills. *The Sociological Imagination.* New York:
Oxford University Press, 1959.

SP   C. Wright Mills. *Sociology and Pragmatism: The Higher Learning
in America,* ed. Irving Louis Horowitz. New York: Oxford
University Press, 1966.

TM   C. Wright Mills. *The Marxists.* New York: Dell Publishing
Company, 1962.

Tovarich   C. Wright Mills. *Tovarich: Contacting the Enemy.* Unpublished.

WC   C. Wright Mills. *White Collar.* New York: Oxford University
Press, 1951.

NOTES

Chapter One: Introduction

1. What I have labelled German sociology is essentially that classical tradition which came out of the shift in nineteenth-century Germany from an historical to a sociological perspective. Its primary emphasis was upon interpretive understanding, and it was basically an historical sociology, which did not claim to discover laws or any unilinear development of mankind. Its major concern was the historical uniqueness of Western civilization and its principal feature, rationalization. The most influential figure associated with this school of thought is Max Weber. For a more detailed discussion, see Raymond Aron, *German Sociology* (New York: The Free Press of Glencoe, 1964).

2. C. Wright Mills, "Letter to the New Left," reprinted as "The New Left," in C. Wright Mills, *Power, Politics and People: The Collected Essays of C. Wright Mills,* Irving Louis Horowitz, ed. (New York: Oxford University Press, 1964), p. 254 (hereafter referred to as PPP).

3. C. Wright Mills, ed., *Images of Man* (New York: George Braziller, Inc., 1960), p. 3 (hereafter referred to as IM).

4. C. Wright Mills, *The Marxists* (New York: Dell Publishing Co., 1962), p. 36 (hereafter referred to as TM). Mills's use of the concept "model" is quite close to William Chambliss's recent formulation. See William Chambliss, ed., *Sociological Readings in the Conflict Perspective* (Reading, Massachusetts: Addison-Wesley Publishing Company, 1973), p. 2.

5. The fact that this working model was first defined in a coauthored work, Hans Gerth and C. Wright Mills, *Character and Social Structure* (New

York: Harcourt, Brace, and World, 1953; Harbinger Books, 1964) (here-after referred to as CSS) and was published after Mills had completed three books and dozens of articles, does not lessen its importance for an under-standing of Mills's sociological theory. Fragments of it can be seen in these early works, and the whole model can be extrapolated from the general corpus of Mills's writings. Also, for the purposes of clarity, only Mills will be referred to in relation to *Character and Social Structure* and to the model. This in no way implies that Mills's contribution to CSS is in any way greater than Gerth's; indeed it is usually next to impossible to assess the relative contributions of a coauthor to a particular work. It is only be-cause I am primarily concerned with Mills that I refer only to him in con-nection with CSS. (Subsequent page citations will be from the 1964 edi-tion.)

6.   C. Wright Mills, *The New Men of Power* (New York: Harcourt, Brace and Company, 1948) (hereafter referred to as NMP). It should be pointed out, though, that NMP developed out of a Columbia University Bureau of Applied Research study that Mills directed as part of his position as vice-director of the bureau at this time, and the theoretical and political parts are incidental to the statistical analysis of the top labor leaders of Ameri-ca. *Puerto Rican Journey,* which Mills coauthored with Clarence Senior and Ruth K. Goldsen (New York: Russell and Russell Company, 1950), also developed out of Mills's affiliation with the Bureau of Applied Research.

7.   C. Wright Mills, "The Social Role of the Intellectual," in PPP, p. 292.

8.   Irving Louis Horowitz, "The Intellectual Genesis of C. Wright Mills," introduction to C. Wright Mills, *Sociology and Pragmatism: The Higher Learning in America* (New York: Oxford University Press, 1966), pp. 13-14. (hereafter referred to as SP).

9.   CSS, p. 10.

10.   C. Wright Mills, *Tovarich: Contacting the Enemy,* unpublished manu-script, unpaginated.

11.   See Robert Friedrichs, *A Sociology of Sociology* (New York: The Free Press, 1970) and Alvin W. Gouldner, *The Coming Crisis of Western Sociology* (New York: Basic Books, Inc., 1970).

12.   Gouldner, *The Coming Crisis of Western Sociology,* p. 6.

Chapter Two: C. Wright Mills—A Biographical Sketch

1.   After the publication of *The Power Elite* (1956) Mills was never able to secure a major research grant. The only grant he received was for a thousand dollars from the Fund for the Republic.

2.   Mills did, however, feel that his father influenced him when it came

to religion. Mills wrote: "My father was a Catholic only for my mother's sake—and although he was not an educated man, he was and is the most honest man I have ever known. Early on I got the idea he didn't believe in it. He never said so; all he said was, 'Son, I just don't know, I really don't,' puzzled like. His puzzlement was enough for me; it did not take." *Tovarich.* Mills liked to refer to himself as a pagan.

3.   Mrs. Yaroslava Mills jokingly told me that "it was tough to live with someone who thought he was always right, not only in political matters but in everything. You know though," she added, smiling, "it most always turned out that he was."

4.   *Tovarich.*

5.   *Ibid.*

6.   *Ibid.*

7.   Although Mills had other coauthors, he never had as intensive and satisfying an intellectual relationship as he had with Gerth.

8.   *Tovarich.*

9.   It is interesting to note that in a 1942 article, "Collectivism and the Mixed-Up Economy," Mills almost prophesied the government's guaranteeing of a loan to the aircraft industry some thirty years later. Mills wrote: "A mixed economy would probably result in the governmental side subsidizing the rise and defaults of the private enterprise side, running around with a net to catch the daring young risk-taker's enterprises every time he is about to fall, break his neck and mash the whole damn audience." In PPP, pp. 184–185.

10.   This is reprinted in PPP as "The Social Role of the Intellectual," pp. 292–304.

11.   Another myth about Mills states that he disliked children. Actually like most men of that time he simply could not cope with little babies and left this to his wife. When the child was older and was talking, Mills was no different from any other father who dutifully reads to his child. Perhaps he even went further than most, because as he read to his child he would translate the story into a more real setting than the typical animal ones found in children's story books. He always believed that children liked to be treated in an intelligent manner.

12.   Dan Wakefield, "Taking It Big," *Atlantic,* Vol. 228, No. 3 (September, 1971), p. 70.

13.   Alvin Gouldner has recently been chided by reviewers for perpetuating this myth in *The Coming Crisis of Western Sociology,* p. 15. Gouldner omits this error in the paperback issue of the book.

14.   Shortly after the reviews of *The Power Elite* were in, Mills wrote an answer to his critics in *Dissent.* He answered most of the criticisms and closed the piece by stating that none of the criticisms had made him modify his

power elite thesis one iota. This article is reprinted in G. William Domhoff and Hoyt B. Ballard, eds., *C. Wright Mills and "The Power Elite"* (Boston: Beacon Press, 1968), pp. 229–250.

15. Saul Landau, "C. Wright Mills: The Last Six Months," *Ramparts,* Vol. 4, No. 4 (August, 1965), p. 49.

16. Harvey Swados, "C. Wright Mills: A Personal Memoir," *Dissent,* Vol. 10, No. 1 (Winter, 1963), p. 42.

17. Mills was particularly interested in visiting China, another way in which he was well ahead of his time.

Chapter Three: Influences upon Mills

1. Don Martindale, *The Nature and Types of Sociological Theory* (Boston, Houghton Mifflin Co., 1960), p. 370.

2. Charles Morris, Introduction to George Herbert Mead, *Mind, Self, and Society* (Chicago: University of Chicago Press, 1934), p. xxii.

3. Mead, *Mind, Self, and Society,* p. 44.

4. George Herbert Mead, *George Herbert Mead on Social Psychology,* edited by Anselm Strauss (Chicago: Phoenix Books, 1964), pp. 214–215.

5. *Ibid.,* p. 218.

6. A. H. Somjee, *The Political Theory of John Dewey* (New York: Columbia University, Teachers College Press, 1968), p. 114.

7. CSS, p. xvii.

8. C. Wright Mills and Patricia J. Salter, "The Barricade and the Bedroom," *Politics,* Vol. 2, No. 10 (October, 1945), p. 314.

9. CSS, p. 44.

10. Erich Fromm, *Man for Himself* (New York: Rinehart and Co., Inc., 1947), p. 241.

11. Although the term *significant other* is usually attributed to George Herbert Mead, it is not found in his works. Mills borrowed the term from Sullivan. For Sullivan's use of the term, see Harry Stack Sullivan, *Conceptions of Modern Psychiatry* (New York: W. W. Norton Co., Inc.), 1953.

12. C. Wright Mills, "Language, Logic and Culture," in PPP, p. 427.

13. Mills used the term *character structure* as a part of the whole and as a descriptive term for the whole itself.

14. CSS, p. 10.

15. CSS, p. 70.

16. Max Weber, *The Theory of Social and Economic Organization,* edited with an introduction by Talcott Parsons (New York: The Free Press, 1964), p. 88.

17. *Ibid.,* p. 118.

18. Julien Freund, *The Sociology of Max Weber* (New York: Random House, 1968), p. 119.

19. Max Weber, *From Max Weber: Essays in Sociology,* translated with an introduction by H. Gerth and C. Wright Mills (New York: Galaxy Books, 1958), p. 73.

20. Weber, *Theory of Social and Economic Organization,* p. 250.

21. See Talcott Parsons's note concerning Weber's failure to develop the concept of occupation in Weber, *Theory of Social and Economic Organization.*

22. Karl Mannheim, *Man and Society in an Age of Reconstruction,* p. 17.

23. *Ibid.,* p. 178.

24. *Ibid.,* p. 184.

25. C. Wright Mills, quoted in Herbert Aptheker, *The World of C. Wright Mills* (New York: Marzoni and Munsell Publishers, 1960), p. 7.

26. TM, p. 22.

27. Landau, "C. Wright Mills: The Last Six Months," p. 50.

28. Mills, "Letter to the New Left," in PPP, p. 257.

29. TM, p. 93.

30. While it is interesting to speculate how Mills might have reacted to the recent publication of the young, humanistic Marx, Mills, while he was alive, considered Marx to be an economic determinist.

31. Irving Louis Horowitz, "The Dragons of Marxism," *The American Scholar,* Vol. 31, No. 4 (Fall, 1962), p. 647.

32. TM, p. 99.

Chapter Four: "Character and Social Structure"

1. Mills used this working model concept as early as 1940 in a review of Karl Mannheim's *Man and Society in an Age of Reconstruction, American Sociological Review,* Vol. 5, No. 6 (December, 1940), pp. 965–969. Here he writes: "There are implicit in the book several considered views of sociological analysis. One is the constructing of working models of various social structures in their totality, typological models into which specific researches may be fitted. Such hypothetical models would overcome the partial perspectives due to ill-advised specialization" (p. 966).

2. CSS, p. 11.

3. CSS, p. 13.

4. CSS, p. 14.

5. Martindale, *Nature and Types of Sociological Theory,* p. 372.

6. CSS, p. 85.

7. Weber, *Theory of Social and Economic Organization,* p. 98.

8. Mills, "Situated Actions and Vocabularies of Motive," in PPP, pp. 447–448.
9. CSS, pp. 179–180.
10. CSS, pp. 278–286.
11. CSS, p. 370.
12. Elliot G. Mishler, review of *Character and Social Structure*, in *Public Opinion Quarterly*, Vol. 18, No. 3 (Fall, 1954), p. 325.
13. Ernest Becker, "Mills' Social Psychology and the Great Historical Convergence on the Problem of Alienation," in Irving Louis Horowitz, ed., *The New Sociology: Essays in Social Science and Social Theory in Honor of C. Wright Mills* (New York: Oxford University Press, 1965), p. 112.
14. Although Dennis Wrong does not specifically single out Mills in his famous article, his criticism of social theorists is quite similar to Becker's. See Dennis H. Wrong, "The Oversocialized Conception of Man in Modern Sociology," *American Sociological Review*, Vol. 26, No. 2 (April, 1961), pp. 183–193; and "Human Nature and the Perspective of Sociology," *Social Research*, Vol. 30, No. 3 (Autumn, 1963), pp. 300–318.

Chapter Five: The Sociology of Knowledge

1. "The Professional Ideology of Social Pathologists" was first published in the *American Journal of Sociology* in 1943; it was originally written as a requirement for a graduate course at the University of Wisconsin.
2. See Irving Louis Horowitz, introduction to SP, p. 15.
3. *Ibid.*
4. Peter Berger and Thomas Luckmann, *The Social Construction of Reality* (New York: Anchor Books, 1966) is a recent exception.
5. Werner Stark, *The Sociology of Knowledge* (London: Routledge and Kegan Paul, 1958), pp. 325–326.
6. *Ibid.*, p. 300.
7. Gunther W. Remmling, *Road to Suspicion: A Study of Modern Mentality and the Sociology of Knowledge* (New York: Appleton-Century-Crofts, 1967), p. 104.
8. Stark, *Sociology of Knowledge*, p. 338.
9. Karl Mannheim, *Essays on the Sociology of Knowledge*, Paul Kecskemeti, ed. (New York: Oxford University Press, 1952), pp. 128–129.
10. Stark, *Sociology of Knowledge*, p. 325.
11. Mills, "Methodological Consequences of the Sociology of Knowledge," in PPP, p. 463. Although this statement may appear tautological at first, it

is not; it serves to introduce the notion that ideology affects the choice of models. Mills, did not, however, fully develop this position until much later, in particular in *The Sociological Imagination* (New York: Oxford University Press, 1959) (hereafter referred to as SI), and "The Cultural Apparatus," in PPP.

12. Mills, "Language, Logic and Culture," in PPP, pp. 425–426.
13. Charles Sanders Peirce, "What Pragmatism Is," in *Pragmatic Philosophy*, Amelie Rorty, ed. (New York: Anchor Books, 1966), p. 21.
14. Mills, "Language, Logic and Culture," in PPP, p. 432.
15. Mills, "Situated Actions and Vocabularies of Motive," in PPP, p. 439.
16. PPP, p. 447.
17. Mills, "The Language and Ideas of Ancient China," in PPP, p. 492.
18. PPP, p. 506. It must be noted that Mills's analysis of Granet is questionable in the light of later research, especially that of Joseph Needham, *Science and Civilization in China* (Cambridge, England: Cambridge University Press, 1954). However, in fairness to Mills, he did write on Granet while still a graduate student and never considered the article publishable. Irving Louis Horowitz included it in PPP. The importance of "The Language and Ideas of Ancient China" for our purposes lies in Mills's embracing a relativistic position on science and rationality.
19. Peirce, "The Fixation of Belief," in Rorty, ed., *Pragmatic Philosophy*, p. 10.
20. I have simplified the differences between Peirce's and Dewey's conceptions of truth. I have also dealt with Dewey's position in greater detail, since Dewey was a far greater influence on Mills than was Peirce. I have also excluded William James's notions of truth from the discussion in this chapter, because his views were quite different from Dewey's and Peirce's, and he also had little or no influence upon Mills's thought in this area. For a more thorough explication of Peirce's position, see W. B. Gallie, *Peirce and Pragmatism* (Middlesex, England: Penquin Books, 1952). For a criticism of Peirce, see John Dewey, *Logic: The Theory of Inquiry* (New York: Henry Holt and Company, 1938), and Bertrand Russell, *Philosophical Essays* (New York: Simon and Schuster, 1966). Dewey's thesis of truth, that of "warranted assertion," is found in John Dewey, *Context and Thought* (Berkeley: University of California Press, 1931). For a critique of this position, though I would call it a misguided one, see Bertrand Russell, "Dewey's Logic," in *The Philosophy of John Dewey*, Phillip A. Schlipp, ed. (Chicago: Northwestern University Press, 1939), pp. 137–156.
21. Peirce, "How to Make Our Ideas Clear," in Rorty, ed., *Pragmatic Philosophy*, p. 17.
22. Jerome Nathanson, *John Dewey* (New York: Charles Scribner's Sons, 1951), p. 47.

23. John Dewey, *The Quest for Certainty* (New York: Minton, Balch and Co., 1928), p. 264.
24. *Ibid.*, p. 197.
25. Somjee, *Political Theory of John Dewey*, pp. 151–152.
26. Mills, "Methodological Consequences," in PPP, p. 464.
27. PPP, p. 468.
28. Mills, "The Professional Ideology of the Social Pathologists," in PPP, pp. 530–531.
29. Here I disagree emphatically with Peter Berger and Thomas Luckmann, who conclude that "C. Wright Mills dealt with the sociology of knowledge in his early writings . . . in an expositional manner and without contributing to its theoretical development." Berger and Luckmann, *Social Construction of Reality*, p. 11. For a recent work which, although coming to a different conclusion concerning Mills's extension of Mannheim's sociology of knowledge, stresses Mills's seminal thinking in the field of the sociology of knowledge, see Derek L. Phillips, "Epistemology and The Sociology of Knowledge: The Contributions of Mannheim, Mills, and Merton," *Theory and Society*, Vol. 1 (1974), pp. 59–84.
30. SP, p. 35.
31. SP, p. 325.
32. SP, p. 418–419.
33. Horowitz, introduction to SP, p. 30.
34. At the time of his death one of Mills's unfinished projects was a comparative study of intellectuals, tentatively titled *The Cultural Apparatus.*
35. Mills, "The Cultural Apparatus," in PPP, pp. 406–407.
36. PPP, P. 409.
37. PPP, p. 410.

Chapter Six: Social Stratification: Occupation, Class, Status, Power, and Powerlessness

1. Mills, "The Sociology of Stratification," in PPP, p. 306. (This article also forms the basis for the chapter on stratification in CSS.)
2. PPP, p. 307.
3. The two exceptions are Hans Gerth and C. Wright Mills, "A Marx for the Managers," *Ethics: An International Journal of Legal, Political and Social Thought;* Vol. 52, No. 2 (January, 1942), pp. 200–215; and C. Wright Mills; "The American Business Elite: A Collective Portrait," *The Journal of Economic History*, Vol. 4, No. 4, Supplement 5 (December, 1945), pp. 20–44. (Both articles are reprinted in PPP.)
4. Swados, "C. Wright Mills: A Personal Memoir," p. 39. For a biographical study of the young Mills during this period, see Richard Gillam, "The

Intellectual as Rebel: C. Wright Mills, 1916-1946," unpublished master's thesis, Columbia University, 1966. For an overall view of this period from the perspective of an intellectual historian, see Christopher Lasch, *The New Radicalism in America 1889-1963* (New York: Alfred A. Knopf, 1965), pp. 286-334.

5. Mills, "The Political Gargoyles: Business as Power," in PPP, p. 75.

6. Mills, "The New Left," in PPP, p. 256.

7. Horowitz, introduction to SP, p. 12.

8. Mills, NMP, p. 252.

9. This advocacy of a program even when he believed it would most likely go unheeded is also found in C. Wright Mills, *The Causes of World War III* (New York: Ballantine Books, 1960) and can only be accounted for by Mills's tenacious belief in the pragmatist's assumption that reason could lead to freedom.

10. NMP, p. 291.

11. Mills outlines the need for finding this link in "The Middle Classes in Middle Sized Cities" (1946), reprinted in PPP, p. 275, where he states: "Properly designated studies in stratification will use both objective and subjective criteria: indeed, one of the key problems of stratification theory is to account for such discrepancies as may thus appear."

12. The emphasis upon CSS, of which Mills was the junior author, and the exclusion of *Puerto Rican Journey,* of which Mills was the senior author, is not an inconsistency. Mills's stamp is obvious in CSS. One has only to look at the sections on stratification, vocabulary of motives, and language, to cite just a few areas, to see that their origin lay in previously published articles by Mills. In *Puerto Rican Journey* this Millsian flavor is lacking.

13. For a different interpretation, see Ralf Dahrendorf, *Class and Class Conflict in Industrial Society* (Stanford, California: Stanford University Press, 1959). Dahrendorf labels Mills a conservative interpreter of Marx while calling James Burnham a radical interpreter.

14. Mills's first wife, Mrs. Alan James, stated that Mills did not read Marx thoroughly until much later. Gillam, "Intellectual as Rebel," p. 38. Mills himself wrote in *Tovarich* that he was more interested in philosophy than politics in the 1930's.

15. Mrs. James also stated that Mills voted for Norman Thomas for president in 1940. Gillam, "Intellectual as Rebel." Dennis H. Wrong, a former student of Mills, related in private correspondence to this writer that Mills was, in the 1940's at least, a fellow-traveller of the Trotskyists (Max Schactman's Socialist Workers Party, the Schactmanites). Mills also wrote in a 1942 article: "I do not see why the aims of socialism need not be quite identical with the aims of classical democracy." C. Wright Mills,

"Collectivism and the Mixed-Up Economy," in PPP, p. 180.

16. Gerth and Mills, "A Marx for the Managers," in PPP, p. 63.

17. PPP, p. 71.

18. C. Wright Mills, "Review of W. Lloyd Warner and Paul Lunt, *The Social Life of a Modern Community*," in PPP, pp. 39-52.

19. C. Wright Mills, "The Nazi Behemoth," in PPP, p. 178.

20. C. Wright Mills, "The Political Gargoyles: Business as Power," in PPP, p. 72.

21. In "Intellectuals: The Powerless People," reprinted in PPP as "The Social Role of the Intellectual," pp. 292-304, Mills is only beginning to find the locus of power; hence his view of who the decision makers are in American society is undeveloped.

22. PPP, p. 294.

23. PPP, pp. 301-302.

24. PPP, p. 304.

25. NMP, p. 25.

26. CSS, p. 328.

27. Mills, "The Sociology of Stratification," in PPP, p. 318.

28. Mills, "The Middle Classes in Middle Sized Cities," in PPP, pp. 274-291. It is interesting to note that this 1946 article was one of the first community power studies. Mills, of course, abandoned this orientation and focused upon the national level.

29. C. Wright Mills, *White Collar: The American Middle Classes* (New York: Oxford University Press, 1951), p. xx (hereafter referred to as WC).

30. WC, p. 3.

31. WC, p. 5.

32. WC, p. 21.

33. WC, p. 71.

34. WC, p. 102.

35. This is the same method Mills used in *The Power Elite*. Most of his critics failed to see this—hence some of the misunderstanding surrounding this work.

36. WC, p. 132.

37. WC, pp. 159-160.

38. WC, pp. 178-179.

39. WC, p. 179.

40. WC, p. 225.

41. WC, p. 325.

42. WC, p. 333.

43. Davis Riesman, review of *White Collar*, in *American Journal of Sociology*, Vol. 58, No. 5 (March, 1952), p. 515.

44.   See Joseph Scimecca and Roland Damiano, *Crisis at St. John's: Strike and Revolution on the Catholic Campus* (New York: Random House, 1968).

45.   Mills himself considered *White Collar* his best work.

Chapter Seven: Power: Period III

1.   For a statement of Mills's three-part conception of power, see "The Structure of Power in American Society," in PPP, pp. 23–38.

2.   C. Wright Mills, *The Power Elite* (New York: Oxford University Press, 1956), p. 9 (hereafter referred to as PE). This definition of power is the same as that used by Max Weber.

3.   PE, p. 18.

4.   PE, p. 141.

5.   PE, p. 193.

6.   PE, p 7.

7.   For an opposing view—one in which technology is seen as defining power through a "technostructure," see John Kenneth Galbraith, *The New Industrial State* (Boston: Houghton-Mifflin and Co., 1967).

8.   Daniel Bell, "The Power Elite Reconsidered," in Domhoff and Ballard, *C. Wright Mills and "The Power Elite,"* pp. 200–201. Bell's article, a number of other criticisms, and Mills's reply to certain critics are reprinted in this work.

9.   Robert A. Dahl, *Modern Political Analysis* (Englewood Cliffs, New Jersey: Prentice-Hall, 1963), p. 34.

10.   C. Wright Mills, "Comments on Criticism," in Domhoff and Ballard, *C. Wright Mills and "The Power Elite,"* p. 240.

11.   G. William Domhoff, *"The Power Elite* and Its Critics," in *ibid.*, p. 277.

12.   PE, p. 164.

13.   Nelson W. Polsby, *Community Power and Political Theory* (New Haven: Yale University Press, 1962), pp. 103–104.

14.   See especially Talcott Parsons, "The Distribution of Power in American Society," in Domhoff and Ballard, *C. Wright Mills and "The Power Elite,"* pp. 60–88.

15.   For an excellent summary of the argument for elite decision making at the presidential level, see Kenneth Prewitt and Alan Stone, *The Ruling Elites: Elite Theory, Power and American Democracy* (New York: Harper and Row, 1973), pp. 105–106.

16.   A. A. Berle, "Are the Blind Leading the Blind?" in Domhoff and

Ballard, *C. Wright Mills and "The Power Elite,"* pp. 97-98. See also Morris Janowitz, ed., *The Professional Soldier* (Glencoe, Illinois: The Free Press, 1960); and Arnold Rose, *The Power Structure* (New York: Oxford University Press, 1967).

17. Prewitt and Stone, *Ruling Elites,* p. 101.

18. C. W. Borklund, *Men of the Pentagon* (New York: Praeger, 1966), p. 219.

19. See Bell, "The Power Elite Reconsidered"; Dahl, *Modern Political Analysis;* and Richard C. Rovere, "The Interlocking Overlappers," in Domhoff and Ballard, *C. Wright Mills and "The Power Elite,"* pp. 172-189.

20. Bell, "The Power Elite Reconsidered," p. 198.

21. A double standard seems to be quite prevalent among pluralists. For an analysis of how pluralists use a double standard when looking at the relationship of the upper class and lower class to power, see Michael J. Parenti, "Power and Pluralism: A View from the Bottom," *Journal of Politics,* Vol. 32, No. 3 (August, 1970), pp. 501-520.

22. William Kornhauser, "'The Power Elite' or 'Veto Groups'?" in Domhoff and Ballard, *C. Wright Mills and "The Power Elite,"* p. 32.

23. A recent case in point concerns Nelson Polsby's review of Domhoff's *Who Rules America?* (Englewood Cliffs, New Jersey: Prentice-Hall, 1968) for the *American Sociological Review.* Domhoff's work, which seeks to graft a Marxist or ruling-class analysis onto Mills's power elite thesis, was the recipient of vitriol not usually seen in this staid professional journal. Little if anything is stated about the book, as Polsby piles up ridicule upon ridicule. Take for instance the cuteness of the following: "Sociologists who missed the book may have caught the movie which starred Jennifer Jones." Nelson W. Polsby, review of G. William Domhoff, *Who Rules America?,* in *American Sociological Review,* Vol. 33, No. 3 (June, 1968), pp. 476-477.

I disagree with Domhoff on a number of points, and I believe Mills's power elite thesis suffers from a mix with Marxist analysis; nevertheless, Domhoff does have something to say about power in America. But Domhoff is not a pluralist and—even worse—is not a sociologist but a psychologist; he is therefore fair game for the academic double standard.

24. See William Connolly, ed., *The Bias of Pluralism* (New York: Atherton Press, 1969).

25. Robert Kennedy, *Thirteen Days* (New York: W. W. Norton and Co., Inc., 1969), and Dean Acheson, *Present at the Creation* (New York: W. W. Norton and Co., Inc., 1969).

26. Robert A. Dahl, *A Preface to Democratic Theory* (Chicago: University of Chicago Press, 1956), p. 151.

27. Floyd Hunter, *Community Power Structure* (Chapel Hill: University

of North Carolina Press, 1953), and *Top Leadership: U. S. A.* (Chapel Hill: University of North Carolina Press, 1959).

28. Rose, *Power Structure,* p. 39.
29. *Ibid.,* p. 381.
30. *Ibid.,* p. 461.
31. *Ibid.,* pp. 476–477.
32. Robert S. Lynd, "Power in the United States," in Domhoff and Ballard, *C. Wright Mills and "The Power Elite,"* p. 107.
33. Aptheker, *The World of C. Wright Mills,* p. 16.
34. PE, p. 324.
35. Aptheker, *The World of C. Wright Mills,* pp. 20-21.
36. In an unpublished manuscript, "Race, Religion—Miscellaneous Opinions and Experiences," in *Tovarich,* Mills wrote: "I have never been interested in what is called the 'Negro Problem.' I have the feeling that if I did look into this problem as a researcher, it would turn out to be a white problem."
37. Paul M. Sweezy, "Power Elite or Ruling Class," in Domhoff and Ballard, *C. Wright Mills and "The Power Elite,"* p. 129.
38. Mills, "Comments on Criticism," p. 244.
39. *Ibid.,* pp. 248-249
40. For an analysis of co-optation in Mills's power scheme, see Domhoff, *Who Rules America?,* chapter one. For a general analysis of co-optation in a large organizational setting, see Robert Presthus, *The Organizational Society* (New York: Vintage Books, 1965).
41. Andrew Hacker, "Power to Do What," in Horowitz, ed., *The New Sociology,* p. 143.

Chapter Eight: The Sociological Imagination and Its Uses

1. See Ernest Becker, *The Lost Science of Man* (New York: George Braziller, Inc., 1971), pp. 145-152. Irving Louis Horowitz has called Mills's method "prescriptivism" in "An Introduction to C. Wright Mills," in PPP, p. 3.
2. SI, p. 171.
3. Prior to the publication of *The Sociological Imagination,* Mills was still considered to be a major sociologist by his peers. *The New Men of Power* and *White Collar* had established his scholarly reputation. These works, particularly *White Collar,* forced America's social scientists to consider *The Power Elite* seriously. Indeed, much of the initial reaction to *The Power Elite* noted that Mills was a respectable academician and there- fore, unlike "Marxists" and other "radicals," had to be taken seriously.

The Causes of World War III, of course, signalled a major break with academic respectability, but even here Mills referred to the book as a pamphlet, indicating that he knew quite well the distinctions between scholarship and polemics. With *The Sociological Imagination*, however, Mills broke with the genteel academic tradition and launched personal attacks on such figures as Talcott Parsons and Paul Lazarsfeld.

4.　SI, pp. 149–150.

5.　SI, p. 158.

6.　SI, pp. 161–162.

7.　SI, p. 165.

8.　The two articles are reprinted in PPP.

9.　Mills, "IBM Plus Reality Plus Humanism = Sociology," in PPP, p. 572.

10.　Dennis Wrong, "The Failure of American Sociology," *Commentary*, Vol. 28, No. 5 (November, 1959), p. 377.

11.　SI, pp. 44–45.

12.　SI, pp. 52–53.

13.　SI, p. 105.

14.　John Dewey, *Human Nature and Conduct* (New York: Henry Holt and Company, 1922), p. 41.

15.　SP, pp. 452–453.

16.　SP, pp. 426–445.

17.　C. Wright Mills, "The Decline of the Left," in PPP, pp. 232–233.

18.　C. Wright Mills, "Public Opinion and Mass Media," in PPP, p. 577.

19.　*Tovarich.*

20.　C. Wright Mills, "Liberal Values in the Modern World," in PPP, p. 189.

21.　TM, pp. 28–29.

22.　For a work which tries to do just this with Marx's model, see Dahrendorf, *Class and Class Conflict in Industrial Society.*

23.　TM, pp. 124–125.

24.　TM, pp. 91–92.

25.　TM, p. 93.

26.　Mills, "Culture and Politics," in PPP, pp. 236–245.

27.　Horowitz, "An Introduction to the New Sociology," in Horowitz, ed., *The New Sociology*, p. 44.

Chapter Nine: Paying Homage to the Father: C. Wright Mills and Radical Sociology

1.　For a description of what constitutes "radical sociology," see J. David Colfax and Jack L. Roach, eds., *Radical Sociology* (New York: Basic Books, Inc., 1971); and Steven Deutsch and John R. Howard, eds., *Where It's At: Radical Perspectives in Sociology* (New York: Harper and Row, 1970).

2. Mills, "The Professional Ideology of Social Pathologists," and SI.

3. PE, *The Causes of World War III; Listen, Yankee;* and TM.

4. For exceptions which seem to be heading in this direction see the recent work of the Frankfurt school—in particular, its leading theorist Jürgen Habermas, *Toward a Rational Society* (Boston: Beacon Press, 1971); *Knowledge and Human Interests* (Boston: Beacon Press, 1972); and *Theory and Practice* (Boston: Beacon Press, 1974). For an introduction to the Frankfurt school, see Trent Schroyer, "Toward a Critical Theory for Advanced Industrial Society," in Hans Peter Dreitzel, ed., *Recent Sociology*, No. 2 (New York: The MacMillan Company, 1970), pp. 210-234. For an American sociologist, see Richard Quinney, *Critique of Legal Order* (Boston: Little, Brown and Company, 1974).

5. Steven E. Deutsch, "The Radical Perspective in Sociology," *Sociological Inquiry*, 40 (Winter, 1970), p. 90.

6. George Gurwitsch's definition reads: "Sociology is the science of human freedom and of all the obstacles which this freedom encounters and overcomes in part." Quoted in Paul Filmer, Michael Phillipson, David Silverman, and David Walsh, *New Directions in Sociological Theory* (Cambridge, Massachusetts: The MIT Press, 1973), p. 124.

7. Gouldner, *The Coming Crisis of Western Sociology.*

8. See for example, Lewis Coser, *The Functions of Social Conflict* (Glencoe, Illinois: The Free Press, 1956).

9. Ralf Dahrendorf, *Essays in the Theory of Society* (Stanford, California: Stanford University Press, 1968); John Rex and Robert Moore, *Race, Community and Conflict* (London: Oxford University Press, 1967).

10. For an analysis of the phenomena in the works of conflict theorists in general, see Dick Atkinson, *Orthodox Consensus and Radical Alternative* (London: Heinemann Educational Books, Ltd., 1971).

11. Dahrendorf, *Essays,* pp. 56-57.

12. Gouldner, *The Coming Crisis of Western Sociology,* p. 382.

13. *Ibid.,* p. 379.

14. The two branches can also be called critical idealists and orthodox Marxists, and other terms can be substituted. For example, Alvin Gouldner refers to the two schools as "critical Marxists" and "scientific Marxists." See Alvin Gouldner, "The Two Marxisms," in Alvin Gouldner, *For Sociology* (New York: Basic Books, 1973), pp. 425-462. What is important is not how they are referred to but the basic contradictory premises they hold.

15. See for example Herbert Marcuse, "Contributions to a Phenomenology of Historical Materialism," *Telos,* 4 (Fall, 1969), pp. 3-34; and Enzo Paci, *The Function of the Sciences and the Meaning of Man* (Evanston, Illinois: Northwestern University Press, 1972).

16.   Al Szymanski, "Marxism and Science," *Insurgent Sociologist,* 3 (Spring, 1973), pp. 27–28.

17.   William Ryan, *Blaming the Victim* (New York: Vintage Books, 1971).

18.   Al Szymanski, "Marxism or Liberalism: A Response to Pozzuto," *Insurgent Sociologist,* 3 (Summer, 1973), p. 58.

19.   Szymanski, "Marxism and Science," p. 29.

20.   David Walsh, "Sociology and the Social World," in Filmer, Phillipson, Silverman, and Walsh, *New Directions in Sociological Theory,* p. 20.

21.   Richard Pozzuto, "Pre-Marxian Marxism: A Critique of Szymanski's 'Marxism and Science,'" *Insurgent Sociologist,* 3 (Summer, 1973), p. 49.

22.   For an excellent and ambitious attempt, see Paci, *Function of the Sciences.* I would argue that it is unsuccessful.

23.   For an excellent and concise summary of the problem, see Gouldner, "The Two Marxisms," in *For Sociology.*

24.   TM, p. 130.

25.   Becker, "Mills' Social Psychology and the Great Historical Convergence on the Problem of Alienation," p. 112.

26.   SI, p. 174.

27.   SI, p. 169.

28.   For example, Szymanski takes this position: "Free-will implies that men are morally responsible and, hence, that punishment is justified. Prisons are based on this doctrine, together with that of rationality. If men are responsible for their actions, then punishment makes sense. On the other hand, if men are forced to do what they do by the logic of an oppressive society, then punishment and guilt make no sense. The invidious doctrine of free-will is used to justify the most horrendous of human actions against other men in the name of 'justice.' The understanding that men are products of their society is eminently humane in its implications. The worst murderers (such as the one portrayed in the outstanding Chilean film *El Chacal de Naueltoro*), are not 'guilty.' Criminals are not responsible for their actions and its makes absolutely no sense to punish them. They are products of their society. In order to free society of their crime, we must change society." "Marxism or Liberalism," p. 62.

29.   For a whole issue devoted to radical sociology, see *Sociological Inquiry,* 40 (Winter, 1970).

30.   Horowitz, "An Introduction to C. Wright Mills," in PPP, p. 20.

BIBLIOGRAPHY

Acheson, Dean. *Present at the Creation.* New York: W. W. Norton and Co., Inc., 1969.

Allport, Gordon W. "The Historical Background of Modern Social Psychology." In Gardner Lindzey, ed. *Handbook of Social Psychology,* Vol 1. Cambridge, Massachusetts: Addison-Wesley Publishing Company, Inc., 1954, pp. 3–56.

Anderson, C. Arnold, and Harry L. Gracey, "C. Wright Mills' *Power Elite:* A Review Article." *Kentucky Law Journal,* Vol. 22, No. 1 (February, 1957), pp. 32–38.

Antoni, Carlo. *From History to Sociology.* Detroit: Wayne State University Press, 1959.

Aptheker, Herbert. *The World of C. Wright Mills.* New York: Marzoni and Munsell Publishers, 1960.

Aron, Raymond. *German Sociology.* New York: The Free Press of Glencoe, 1964.

Atkinson, Dick. *Orthodox Consensus and Radical Alternative.* London: Heineman Educational Books Ltd., 1971.

Bachrach, Peter. *The Theory of Democratic Elitism: A Critique.* Boston: Little, Brown and Company, 1967.

Becker, Ernest. "Mills' Social Psychology and the Great Historical Convergence on the Problem of Alienation." In Irving Louis Horowitz, ed. *The New Sociology: Essays in Social Science and Social Theory in Honor of C. Wright Mills.* New York: Oxford University Press, 1965, pp. 108–133.

_____. *Beyond Alienation.* New York: George Braziller, 1967.

_____. *The Structure of Evil.* New York: George Braziller, 1968.

_____. *The Lost Science of Man.* New York: George Braziller, 1971.

Berger, Peter L. and Thomas Luckmann. *The Social Construction of Reality.* New York: Doubleday and Company, Inc., 1966.

Bendix, Reinhard. *Max Weber: An Intellectual Portrait.* New York: Doubleday and Company, Inc., 1962.

Bierstedt, Robert. *The Social Order.* New York: McGraw-Hill Book Company, Inc., 1963.

_____. Review of *The Power Elite. Political Science Quarterly,* Vol. 71, No. 4 (December, 1956), pp. 606–607.

_____. "Nominal and Real Definitions in Sociological Theory." In Llewellan Gross, ed. *Symposium on Sociological Theory.* New York: Row, Peterson and Company, 1959, pp. 121–144.

Borklund, C. W. *Men of the Pentagon.* New York: Praeger, 1966.

Bottomore, T. B. *Elites and Society.* Middlesex, England: Penguin Books, 1964.

_____. *Critics of Society.* New York: Pantheon Books, 1968.

Braithwaite, Richard B. *Scientific Explanation.* New York: Harper Torchbooks, 1960.

Burnham, James. *The Managerial Revolution.* New York: John Day Company, Inc., 1941.

Chambliss, William, ed. *Sociological Readings in the Conflict Perspective.* Reading, Massachusetts: Addison-Wesley Publishing Company, 1973.

Colfax, J. David and Jack L. Roach, eds. *Radical Sociology.* New York: Basic Books, 1971.

Connolly, William, ed. *The Bias of Pluralism.* New York: Atherton Press, 1969.

Coser, Lewis. "The Uses of Sociology." *Partisan Review,* Vol. 27, No. 1 (Winter, 1960), pp. 167–173.

Cox, Oliver C. "Max Weber on Social Stratification: A Critique." *American Sociological Review,* Vol. 15, No. 2 (April, 1950), pp. 223–227.

Dahl, Robert A. *A Preface to Democratic Theory.* Chicago: University of Chicago Press, 1956.

_____. *Modern Political Analysis.* Englewood Cliffs, New Jersey: Prentice-Hall, 1963.

Dahrendorf, Ralf. *Class and Class Conflict in Industrial Society.* Stanford, California: Stanford University Press, 1959.

_____. *Essays in the Theory of Society.* Stanford, California: Stanford University Press, 1968.

Deutsch, Steven E. "The Radical Perspective in Sociology." *Sociological Inquiry,* Vol. 40, No. 1 (Winter, 1970), pp. 85–93.

_____, and John Howard, eds. *Where It's At: Radical Perspectives in Sociology.* New York: Harper and Row, 1970.

Dewey, John. *Human Nature and Conduct.* New York: Henry Holt and Company, 1922.

_____. *The Quest for Certainty.* New York: Minton, Balch and Company, 1928.

_____. *Context and Thought.* Berkeley: University of California Press, 1931.

_____. *Logic: The Theory of Inquiry.* New York: Henry Holt and Company, 1938.

_____. *Freedom and Culture.* New York: G. P. Putnam's Sons, 1939.

_____, and Arthur F. Bentley. *Knowing and the Known.* Boston: Beacon Press, 1949.

Domhoff, G. William. *Who Rules America?* Englewood Cliffs, New Jersey: Prentice-Hall, 1968.

_____. *The Higher Circles: The Governing Class in America.* New York: Random House, 1970.

_____. *Fat Cats and Democrats.* Englewood Cliffs, New Jersey: Prentice-Hall, 1972.

_____, and Hoyt B. Ballard, eds. *C. Wright Mills and "The Power Elite."* Boston: Beacon Press, 1968.

Ellul, Jacques. *The Technological Society.* New York: Vintage Books, 1964.

Endleman, Robert, ed. *Personality and Social Life.* New York: Random House, 1967.

Filmer, Paul, Michael Phillipson, David Silverman, and David Walsh. *New Directions in Sociological Theory.* Cambridge, Massachusetts: MIT Press, 1973.

Freund, Julian. *The Sociology of Max Weber.* New York: Pantheon Books, 1968.

Friedrichs, Robert. *A Sociology of Sociology.* New York: The Free Press, 1970.

Fromm, Erich. *Man for Himself.* New York: Holt, Rinehart and Company, 1947.

Galbraith, John Kenneth. *The New Industrial State.* Boston: Houghton Mifflin Company, 1967.

_____. *How to Control the Military.* New York: New American Library, 1969.

Gallie, W. B. *Peirce and Pragmatism.* Middlesex, England: Penguin Books, 1952.

Gamberg, Herbert. "Science and Scientism: The State of Sociology." *The American Sociologist,* Vol. 4, No. 2 (May, 1969), pp. 111–116.

Gardiner, P. L. *The Nature of Historical Explanation.* London: Oxford University Press, 1952.

Geiger, George Raymond. "Dewey's Social and Political Philosophy." In Paul Arthur Schlipp, ed. *The Philosophy of John Dewey.* Chicago: Northwestern University Press, 1939, pp. 335–368.

Gerth, Hans H. "C. Wright Mills, 1916–1962." *Studies on the Left,* Vol 2, No. 3 (Summer, 1962), pp. 7–11.

_____, and C. Wright Mills. "A Marx for the Managers." *Ethics: An International Journal of Legal, Political and Social Thought,* Vol. 52, No. 2 (January, 1942), pp. 200–215.

_____, and _____. *Character and Social Structure.* New York: Harcourt, Brace and World, 1953.

Gillam, Richard. "The Intellectual as Rebel: C. Wright Mills 1916–1946." Unpublished master's thesis, Columbia University, 1966.

Goffman, Erving. *The Presentation of Self in Everyday Life.* Garden City, New York: Doubleday, 1959.

_____. *Encounters.* Indianapolis: The Bobbs-Merrill Company Inc., 1961.

_____. *Behavior in Public Places.* New York: The Free Press, 1963.

_____. *Relations in Public: Microstudies of the Public Order.* New York: Basic Books, Inc., 1971.

Gouldner, Alvin W. *The Coming Crisis of Western Sociology.* New York: Basic Books, Inc., 1970.

_____. "'Varieties of Political Expression' Re-visited." *American Journal of Sociology,* Vol. 78, No. 5 (March, 1973), pp. 1063–1093.

_____. "The Two Marxisms." In *For Sociology*. New York: Basic Books, 1973, pp. 425–462.

Habermas, Jürgen. *Toward a Rational Society*. Boston: Beacon Press, 1971.

_____. *Knowledge and Human Interests*. Boston: Beacon Press, 1972.

_____. *Theory and Practice*. Boston: Beacon Press, 1974.

Halberstam, David. *The Best and the Brightest*. New York: Random House, 1972.

Hardman, J. S. and Maurice Newfeld, eds. *The House of Labor*. New York: Prentice-Hall, 1951.

Hausknecht, Murray. "The Independent Radical." Unpublished master's thesis, Columbia University, 1950.

Horowitz, Irving Louis. "The Sociological Imagination of C. Wright Mills." *American Journal of Sociology*, Vol. 68, No. 1 (July, 1962), pp. 105–107.

_____. "C. Wright Mills and the Dragons of Marxism." *The American Scholar*, Vol. 31, No. 4 (Fall, 1962), pp. 646–652.

_____. "The Unfinished Writings of C. Wright Mills: The Last Phase." *Studies on the Left*, Vol. 3, No. 4 (Fall, 1963), pp. 247–259.

_____. *Professing Sociology: Studies in the Life Cycle of Social Science*. Chicago: Aldine Publishing Company, 1968.

_____, ed. *The New Sociology: Essays in Social Science and Social Theory in Honor of C. Wright Mills*. New York: Oxford University Press, 1965.

Hughes, H. Stuart. *Consciousness and Society*. New York: Random House, 1958.

Hunter, Floyd. *Community Power Structure*. Chapel Hill: University of North Carolina Press, 1953.

_____. *Top Leadership: U. S. A.* Chapel Hill: University of North Carolina Press, 1959.

Janowitz, Morris, ed. *The Professional Soldier*. Glencoe, Illinois: The Free Press, 1960.

Kariel, Henry S. *Open Systems: Arenas for Political Action*. Itasca, Illinois: F. E. Pencock Publishers, Inc., 1969.

Keller, Suzanne. *Beyond the Ruling Class*. New York: Random House, 1968.

Kennedy, Robert. *Thirteen Days*. New York: W. W. Norton and Co., Inc., 1969.

Kolko, Gabriel. *Wealth and Power in America*. New York: Frederick A. Praeger, 1962.

Landau, Saul. "C. Wright Mills: The Last Six Months." *Ramparts*, Vol. 4, No. 4 (August, 1965), pp. 46–54.

Lasch, Christopher. *The New Radicalism in America, 1889–1963*. New York: Alfred A. Knopf, 1965.

_____. *The Agony of the New Left*. New York: Alfred A. Knopf, 1969.

LeFebre, Henri. *The Sociology of Marx*. New York: Pantheon Books, 1968.

Lekachman, Robert. "Organization Men: The Erosion of Individualism." *Commentary*, Vol. 23, No. 3 (March, 1957), pp. 271–276.

Lipset, Seymour Martin, and Neil Smelser. "Change and Controversy in Recent American Sociology." *British Journal of Sociology*, Vol. 12, No. 2 (March, 1961), pp. 41–51.

Lockwood, David. "Social Integration and System Integration." In George K. Zollschen and Walter Hirsh, eds. *Explorations in Social Change*.

Boston: Houghton Mifflin Company, 1964, pp. 244–257.

Lowenstein, Karl. *Max Weber's Political Ideas in the Perspective of Our Time.* Amherst: The University of Massachusetts Press, 1966.

Lundberg, Ferdinand. *America's Sixty Families.* New York: The Vanguard Press, 1937.

_____. *The Rich and the Super-Rich.* New York: Bantam Books, 1968.

Lyman, Stanford M., and Marvin B. Scott. *A Sociology of the Absurd.* New York: Appleton Century Crofts, 1970.

Mannheim, Karl. *Ideology and Utopia.* New York: Harcourt, Brace and World, Inc., 1936.

_____. *Man and Society in an Age of Reconstruction.* New York: Harcourt, Brace and World, Inc., 1940.

_____. *Essays on the Sociology of Knowledge.* Paul Kecskemeti, ed. New York: Oxford University Press, 1952.

Marcuse, Herbert. *One Dimensional Man.* Boston: Beacon Press, 1967.

_____. *Eros and Civilization.* New York: Vintage Books, 1968.

_____. "Contributions to a Phenomenology of Historical Materialism." *Telos,* 4 (Fall, 1969), pp. 3–34.

Martindale, Don. *The Nature and Types of Sociological Theory.* Boston: Houghton Mifflin Company, 1960.

_____. "Limits and Alternatives to Functionalism in Sociology," in *Functionalism in the Social Sciences.* Don Martindale, ed. Monograph 5, The American Academy of Social and Political Science, 1965, pp. 144–162.

Marx, Karl. *Karl Marx: Selected Writings in Sociology and Social Philosophy.* T. B. Bottomore, ed. New York: McGraw-Hill Book Company, 1964.

_____ and Friedrich Engels, *Basic Writings on Politics and Philosophy.* New York: Doubleday and Company, Inc., 1959.

Matson, Floyd W. *The Broken Image.* New York: Doubleday, Anchor Books, 1966.

Mead, George Herbert. *The Philosophy of the Present.* Chicago: Open Court Publishing Company, 1932.

_____. *Mind, Self, and Society.* Charles Morris, ed. Chicago: The University of Chicago Press, 1934.

_____. *George Herbert Mead on Social Psychology.* Anselm Strauss, ed. Chicago: The University of Chicago Press, 1956.

Meadows, Paul. "Models, Systems and Science." *American Sociological Review,* Vol. 22, No. 2 (February, 1957), pp. 3–9.

Melman, Seymour. *Pentagon Capitalism: The Political Economy of War.* New York: McGraw Hill, 1970.

Mills, C. Wright. Review of Karl Mannheim, *Man and Society in an Age of Reconstruction. American Sociological Review,* Vol. 5, No. 6 (December, 1940), pp. 965–969.

_____. Review of Logan Wilson, *The Academic Man. American Sociological Review,* Vol 7, No. 3 (June, 1942), pp. 444–446.

_____. "The Case for the Coal Miners." *The New Republic,* Vol. 108, No. 21 (May 24, 1943), pp. 695–698.

_____. Review of Wilfred E. Binkley, *American Political Parties. The New Leader,* Vol. 26, No. 44 (October 30, 1943), pp. 3, 7.

_____. "The Conscription of America." *Common Sense,* Vol. 14, No. 3 (April, 1945), pp. 15–17.

_____. "A Who's What of Union Leadership." *Labor and Nation,* Vol. 2, No. 3 (December, 1945), pp. 33–36.

_____. "The Politics of Skill." *Labor and Nation,* Vol. 2, No. 6 (June–July, 1946), p. 35.

_____. "What Research Can Do for Labor." *Labor and Nation,* Vol. 2, No. 6 (June–July, 1946), pp. 17–20.

_____. "Five Publics the Polls Don't Catch." *Labor and Nation,* Vol. 3, No. 3 (May–June, 1947), pp. 22–25.

_____. "Grass-Roots Union with Ideas: The Auto Workers——Something New in American Labor." *Commentary,* Vol. 20, No. 3 (March, 1948), pp. 240–247.

_____. *The New Men of Power.* New York: Harcourt, Brace and World, 1948.

_____. "Notes on White Collar Unionism." *Labor and Nation,* Vol. 5, No. 2 (March-April, 1949), pp. 17–21.

_____. Review of Richard Centers, *The Psychology of Social Classes.* *The Annals of the American Association of Political and Social Science,* Vol. 268 (March, 1950), pp. 241–242.

_____. *White Collar.* New York: Oxford University Press, 1951.

_____. Review of Reinhard Bendix, *Higher Civil Servants in American Society.* *American Journal of Sociology,* Vol. 57, No. 5 (March, 1952), p. 523.

_____. "Commentary on Our Culture and Our Country." *Partisan Review,* Vol. 19, No. 4 (July-August, 1952), pp. 446–450.

_____. Review of Floyd Hunter, *Community Power Structure: A Study of Decision Makers. Social Forces,* Vol. 30, No. 1 (October, 1953), p. 92.

_____. *The Power Elite.* New York: Oxford University Press, 1956.

_____. *The Causes of World War III.* New York: Simon and Schuster, Inc., 1958.

_____. "Psychology and Social Science." *Monthly Review,* Vol. 10, No. 6 (October, 1958), pp. 204–209.

_____. *The Sociological Imagination.* New York: Oxford University Press, 1959.

_____. "Crackpot Realism." *Fellowship,* Vol. 25, No. 1 (January, 1959), pp. 3–8.

_____, ed. *Images of Man.* New York: George Braziller, Inc., 1960.

_____. *Listen, Yankee: The Revolution in Cuba.* New York: Ballantine Books, 1960.

_____. "On Latin America, The Left, and the U. S." *Evergreen Review,* Vol. 5, No. 16 (January, 1961), pp. 110–122.

_____. *The Marxists.* New York: Dell Publishing Company, 1962.

_____. *Power, Politics and People: The Collected Essays of C. Wright Mills.* Irving Louis Horowitz, ed. New York: Oxford University Press, 1964.

_____. *Sociology and Pragmatism: The Higher Learning in America.* Irving Louis Horowitz, ed. New York: Oxford University Press, 1966.

_____ and Patricia Salter. "The Barricade and the Bedroom." *Politics,* Vol. 2, No. 10 (October, 1945), pp. 313–315.

_____ (with the assistance of Melville J. Ulmer). *Small Business and*

Civic Welfare. Washington, D. C.: Smaller War Plants Corporation, United States Senate, 1946.

———— and Hazel Gaudet. "What the People Think: Review of Selected Opinion Polls." *Labor and Nation*, Vol. 2, No. 1 (November–December, 1946), pp. 11–13.

———— and Thelma Ehrlich. "The People in the Unions." *Labor and Nation*, Vol. 3, No. 1 (January–February, 1947), pp. 28–31.

———— and Hazel Gaudet Erskine. "What the People Think: Anti-Labor Legislation." *Labor and Nation*, Vol. 3, No. 2 (March–April, 1947), pp. 25–29.

———— and Helen Schneider. "The Political Complexion of Union Leadership." *Labor and Nation*, Vol. 3, No. 4 (July–August, 1947), pp. 11–15.

———— and Helen Schneider. "What Chances of Organic Trade Union Unity?" *Labor and Nation*, Vol. 3, No. 5 (September–October, 1947), pp. 14–16.

————, Clarence Senior, and Ruth K. Goldsen. *Puerto Rican Journey*. New York: Russell and Russell Company, 1950.

Mishler, Elliot G. Review of *Character and Social Structure*. *Public Opinion Quarterly*, Vol. 18, No. 3 (Fall, 1954), pp. 323–326.

Nathanson, Jerome. *John Dewey*. New York: Charles Scribner's Sons, 1951.

Needham, Joseph. *Science and Civilization in China*. Cambridge, England: Cambridge University Press, 1954.

Paci, Enzo. *The Function of the Sciences and the Meaning of Man*. Evanston, Illinois: Northwestern University Press, 1972.

Parenti, Michael J. "Power and Pluralism: A View from the Bottom." *Journal of Politics*, Vol. 32, No. 3 (August, 1970), pp. 501–530.

Parsons, Talcott. *The Social System*. New York: The Free Press, 1964.

———— and Edward Shils, eds. *Toward a General Theory of Action*. New York: Harper and Row Publishers, 1967.

Peirce, Charles Sanders. *The Collected Papers of Charles Sanders Peirce*. Charles Hartshorn and Paul Weiss, eds. Cambridge: Harvard University Press, 1937, Vols. 1 and 2.

————. *Essays in the Philosophy of Science*. Vincent Tomas, ed. Indianapolis: The Bobbs-Merrill Company, 1957.

Pfuetze, Paul. *The Social Self*. New York: Harper Torchbooks, 1961.

Phillips, Derek L. "Epistemology and the Sociology of Knowledge: The Contributions of Mannheim, Mills and Merton." *Theory and Society*, 1 (1974), pp. 59–88.

Polsby, Nelson. *Community Power and Political Theory*. New Haven: Yale University Press, 1963.

————. Review of G. William Domhoff: *Who Rules America? American Sociological Review*, Vol. 33, No. 3 (June, 1968), pp. 476–477.

Popper, Karl. *The Poverty of Historicism*. New York: Harper Torchbooks, 1959.

Pozzuto, Richard. "Pre-Marxian Marxism: A Critique of Szymanski's Marxism and Science." *Insurgent Sociologist*, 3 (Summer, 1973), pp. 48–55.

Presthus, Robert. *The Organizational Society*. New York: Vintage Books, 1965.

Prewitt, Kenneth, and Alan Stone. *The Ruling Elites: Elite Theory, Power and American Democracy.* New York: Harper and Row, 1973.

Quinney, Richard. *The Social Reality of Crime.* Boston: Little Brown and Company, 1970.

_____. *Critique of Legal Order.* Boston: Little, Brown and Company, 1974.

Record, Wilson C. "Of History and Sociology." *American Quarterly,* Vol. 2, No. 3 (Fall, 1959), pp. 425–429.

Remmling, Gunther. *Road to Suspicion: A Study of Modern Mentality and the Sociology of Knowledge.* New York: Appleton Century Crofts, 1967.

Rex, John. *Key Problems in Sociological Theory.* London: Routledge and Kegan Paul, 1961.

_____ and Robert Moore. *Race, Community and Conflict.* London: Oxford University Press, 1967.

Riesman, David. Review of *White Collar. American Journal of Sociology,* Vol. 57, No. 5 (March, 1952), pp. 513–515.

_____, Nathan Glazer, and Reuel Denney. *The Lonely Crowd: A Study of the Changing American Character.* New York: Doubleday and Company Inc., 1963.

Roach, Jack L. "The Radical Sociology Movement: A Short History and Commentary." *The American Sociologist,* Vol. 5, No. 3 (August, 1970), pp. 224–235.

Rorty, Amelie, ed. *Pragmatic Philosophy.* New York: Doubleday, Anchor Books, 1966.

Rose, Arnold. *The Power Structure.* New York: Oxford University Press, 1967.

Russell, Bertrand. "Dewey's Logic." In Phillip A. Schlipp, ed. *The Philosophy of John Dewey.* Chicago: Northwestern University Press, 1939, pp. 137–156.

_____. *Philosophical Essays.* New York: Simon and Schuster, 1966.

Ryan, William. *Blaming The Victim.* New York: Vintage Books, 1971.

Schroyer, Trent. "Toward a Critical Theory for Advanced Industrial Society." In Hans Peter Dreitzel, ed. *Recent Sociology No. 2.* New York: The Macmillan Company, 1970.

Scimecca, Joseph, and Roland Damiano. *Crisis at St. John's: Strike and Revolution on the Catholic Campus.* New York: Random House, 1968.

Selznick, Philip. Review of *Character and Social Structure. American Sociological Review,* Vol. 19, No. 4 (August, 1954), pp. 485–486.

Sharp, G. B. "Mills and Weber: Formalism and the Analysis of Social Structure." *Science and Society,* Vol. 24, No. 2 (Spring, 1960), pp. 113–133.

Sheehan, Neil, Hendrick Smith, W. W. Kenworth, and Fox Butterfield. *The Pentagon Papers.* New York: Bantam Books, 1971.

Shils, Edward A. "Professor Mills on the Calling of Sociology." *World Politics,* Vol. 13, No. 4 (July, 1961), pp. 600–621.

Somjee. A. H. *The Political Theory of John Dewey.* New York: Columbia University, Teachers College Press, 1968.

Spinrad, William. "The Socio-Political Orientations of C. Wright Mills: An Evaluation." *The British Journal of Sociology,* Vol. 17, No. 1 (March, 1966), pp. 45–59.

Stark, Werner. *The Sociology of Knowledge.* London: Routledge and Kegan Paul, 1958.

Sullivan, Harry Stack. *Conceptions of Modern Psychiatry*. New York: W. W. Norton Company, Inc., 1953.

Swados, Harvey. "C. Wright Mills: A Personal Memoir." *Dissent*, Vol. 10, No. 1 (Winter, 1963), pp. 35–42.

Szymanski. Albert. "Toward a Radical Sociology." *Sociological Inquiry*, Vol. 40, No. 1 (Winter, 1970), pp. 3–25.

_____. "Marxism and Science." *Insurgent Sociologist*, 3 (Spring, 1973), pp. 25–38.

_____. "Marxism or Liberalism: A Reply to Pozzuto." *Insurgent Sociologist*, 4 (Summer, 1973), pp. 56–62.

Tumin, Melvin. Review of *Power, Politics and People: The Collected Essays of C. Wright Mills*. *American Sociological Review*, Vol. 29, No. 2 (February, 1964), pp. 123–124.

Van der Berghe, Pierre L. "Dialectic and Functionalism." *American Sociological Review*, Vol. 28, No. 5 (October, 1963), pp. 695–705.

Wakefield, Dan. "Taking It Big: A Memoir of C. Wright Mills." *Atlantic*, Vol. 228, No. 3 (September, 1971), pp. 65–71.

Walker, Jack L. "A Critique of the Elitist Theory of Democracy." *American Political Science Review*, Vol. 605, No. 2 (June, 1966), pp. 285–295.

Weber, Max. *From Max Weber*, H. H. Gerth and C. Wright Mills, eds. New York: Oxford University Press, 1946.

_____. *The Theory of Social and Economic Organization*. Talcott Parsons ed. New York: Oxford University Press, 1947.

_____. *The Protestant Ethic and the Spirit of Capitalism*. New York: Charles Scribner's Sons, 1958.

Whyte, William H., Jr. *The Organization Man*. Garden City, New York: Doubleday Anchor Books, 1956.

Wilhelm, Sidney M. "Elites, Scholars and Sociologists." *Catalyst* (Summer, 1966), pp. 1–10.

Winch, Peter. *The Idea of a Social Science and Its Relation to Philosophy*. London: Routledge and Kegan Paul, 1958.

Wolfe, Robert. *The Poverty of Liberalism*. Boston: Beacon Press, 1968.

Wrong, Dennis H. "Our Troubled Middle Classes." *American Mercury*, Vol. 74, No. 337 (January, 1952), pp. 107–113.

_____. "The Failure of American Sociology." *Commentary*, Vol. 28. No. 5 (November, 1959), pp. 375–380.

_____. "The Over-Socialized Conception of Man in Modern Sociology." *American Sociological Review*, Vol. 26, No. 2 (April, 1961), pp. 183–193.

_____. "Reading from Left to Right." *Partisan Review*, Vol. 30, No. 2 (Summer, 1963), pp. 292–297.

_____. "Human Nature and the Perspective of Sociology." *Social Research*, Vol. 30, No. 3 (Autumn, 1963), pp. 300–318.

_____. "Some Problems in Defining Social Power." *American Journal of Sociology*, Vol. 73, No. 6 (May, 1961), pp. 673–681.

Yarmolinsky, Adam. *The Military Establishment*. New York: Harper and Row Publishers, 1971.

Zeitlin, Irving M. *Marxism: A Re-Examination* Princeton, New Jersey: D. Von Nostrand Company, Inc., 1967.

_____. *Rethinking Sociology*. New York: Meredith Corporation, 1973.

Zeitlin, Maurice. *Revolutionary Politics and the Cuban Working Class*. New York: Harper and Row Publishers, 1970.

INDEX

Joseph Scimecca, Assistant Professor of Sociology and Education at the State University of New York at Albany, has been interested in the work of C. Wright Mills for over a decade. He is coauthor of Crisis at St. John's: Strike and Revolution on the Catholic Campus, *1968.*